A Guide to...
Asiatic Parrots
Their Mutations, Care and Breeding
Revised Edition

By Syd and Jack Smith

Published and Edited by Australian Birdkeeper Publications ©

First Published 1990 by
Australian Birdkeeper Publications
PO Box 6288
South Tweed Heads
NSW 2486 Australia
Reprinted 1992
Revised Edition 1997

ISBN 0 9587102 52

Front Cover:
Top left: Blue Indian Ringnecked cock.
Centre left: Alexandrine Parrot cock.
Bottom left: Plum-headed Parrot cock.
Bottom right: Malabar Parrot cock.
Back Cover:
Australian Pied Indian Ringnecked cock.

Front and back cover photographs
by Syd and Jack Smith.

All photographs in this book are by Syd and Jack Smith,
except where shown.

Design, Type and Art: PrintHouse Multimedia Graphics (Gold Coast)
Colour Separations: NuScan (Gold Coast)
Printing: Prestige Litho (Brisbane)

Contents

Syd Smith

Jack Smith

Authors' Comment

Since writing the first edition of **A Guide to Asiatic Parrots** we have received many favourable comments on its contents from aviculturists within Australia and overseas, which is gratifying to us both.

We hope this revised edition will be as popular. Again we thank our wives, Glad and Gwen, for their support and assistance, allowing our hobby to expand to what it is today.

The many thousands of kilometres we have travelled meeting other fanciers past and present, exchanging ideas and viewing their collections, has been invaluable in increasing the wealth of knowledge for us both and we thank these aviculturists and their families for their hospitality and friendship.

We would particularly like to thank Alan Lynch, Peter Russell and Dr Terry Martin for their assistance in the preparation of this revision.

Finally, we would like to express our thanks to both Nigel and Sheryll of **Australian Birdkeeper Publications** for their assistance in completing this revised edition.

About the Authors

Our background to aviculture began in our younger days when, as boys, we would spend weekends roaming the countryside either rabbiting or bird nesting.

Hours were spent sitting, looking and listening, in the scrub or around water-holes at bird life. There is no doubt we both gained invaluable knowledge from observing bird behaviour.

Returning home when we were hungry, with perhaps young birds, rabbits or snakes, our mother would give us both a good reprimand. She never did get through to us that weekends were for cutting firewood and lawn mowing. After accumulating birds of all descriptions, housed in a conglomeration of netting and fruit cases, our father built our first aviary, a 1.2 metre (4 feet) square box with a wire front, on legs 600mm (2 feet) off the ground. We are still building aviaries today.

Now, having more than 200 breeding flights at Harkaway, situated 43.5km (27 miles) east of Melbourne, Victoria, we are both kept busy after work and at weekends attending to our hobby.

Having kept most parrots that have been available in Australia, except for the Lorikeets and Black Cockatoos, you soon realise that some birds require more attention than others, so it is a matter of the time you have available and what species fit into that schedule.

We know most bird people would like to keep all types of birds, however there is not much point in keeping something if you cannot give the necessary requirements to be successful in breeding.

Asiatic Parrots fit into our life style and time programme and that is why our collection houses so many of this group. Basically, they are hardy, will breed on an easily prepared diet, have a very tight feather pattern which gives them an immaculate appearance, and all breed at a similar time of the year.

Over the years that we have kept Asiatic Parrots there has always been a steady demand from other aviculturists, as nobody can mass produce them by trapping, which can happen with native species.

The basis of this book is to relate our experiences in the housing, management, nutrition and breeding of Asiatic Parrots.

All of the information hereafter has proven to be successful in our overall management regime. If the reader's methodology differs from ours, and is successful, do not change. However, we can all learn from the experiences of others, and we certainly hope that our experiences assist other breeders of this species.

Ceramic figurines as produced by Syd and Jack Smith.

Introduction

K. WILSON

*Alexandrine
Parrot cock.*

Introduction

Asiatic Parrots are all members of the genus *Psittacula*, in which each species shows a ring around the neck. This ring separates the often brightly coloured head from the remainder of the body.

Psittacula ranges widely, with the Ringnecked *Psittacula krameri* being the most vastly distributed of the family.

The Indian subcontinent is the centre of distribution of the family *Psittacula*, having eight of the total genus originating from this region. The Derbyan Parrot, *P. derbyana* is found in China and the Malayan Long-tailed Parrot, *P. longicauda*, is found in Malaya, Sumatra and Borneo.

The avicultural history of *Psittacula* dates back many centuries. In fact, Alexander the Great is attributed with introducing the Alexandrine Parrot, *P. eupatria* to Europe. Descriptions and illustrations of those parrots known to the early Greeks and Romans prior to the time of Nero, are almost always of Ringnecks, either *P. krameri manillensis,* the Indian Ringnecked Parrot, or *P.k. krameri*, the African Ringnecked Parrot.

In the wild, most members of this genus are found in small groups, which congregate in large to enormous flocks to roost, or where food is plentiful. In some areas they are considered as serious pests because of the damage caused to cultivated crops.

These beautiful birds are better known as aviary subjects than as pets. Indeed many individuals looking for a pet bird are immediately taken by the beauty, intelligence and tameness of young Asiatic Parrots. The two largest species of *Psittacula*, the Alexandrine and the Derbyan Parrot, are noted for their intelligence and the Malabar Parrot, *P. columboides*, is an extremely quiet and endearing bird. However, as they age, most will become less tolerant of human attention and some may even turn exceptionally aggressive. If handreared, as most potential pet birds are, they lack all fear and do not hesitate to bite. Another reason for not advocating an Asiatic Parrot for a pet, is their need to fly. If housed in a small cage, as is the case with most pet birds, it would be a cruel life for a bird that in the wild makes so frequent use of its wings and is accustomed to great activity.

Asiatic Parrots are a spectacular family of parrots that have only recently, in avicultural history, been truly appreciated for their virtues and worth as superb aviary specimens.

Malabar cock.

Management

In acquiring birds we prefer to purchase young stock from other breeders whose climate and housing are similar to our own. With

R. LOW

young birds, you may have the problem of not knowing what sex they are, but at least you know they are not culls and have a full life ahead of them. If you obtain birds that have been housed or bred in a different climate to your own, you may have problems acclimatising these birds to your conditions.

All too often, one hears of people obtaining adult breeding pairs, even in the breeding season, that in most cases are only worn out old culls. Certainly, genuine adult birds do come on the market at times, due to various circumstances, however it is advisable to research their background before purchasing such birds.

A good time to purchase stock in Australia, is late December. The breeding season has finished and there is a good choice of young birds on the market. The days are still long and the weather is warm. This gives new arrivals time to settle in and you usually have more time to observe their behaviour in their new aviaries.

A trap many aviculturists fall into is that they do not keep any replacement stock from their own breeding. Fortunately, having plenty of aviary space, we always maintain a few

African Ringnecked cock- note the darker colour of the beak than is seen on an Indian Ringneck.

youngsters for our own use, as one never knows when you may lose a breeder. Some species are difficult to replace and you can spend hours sourcing the right bird.

Handling of Parrots

Every person who keeps birds will have to catch their birds for transfer or despatch at some stage.

Above and right:
Method of holding a parrot without being bitten.

Many birds are damaged or lost during this procedure by unthinking or inexperienced owners.

We use a prawn dip net (available at most fishing tackle stores) to catch our birds in the aviaries.

These nets are approximately 375mm (15 inches) in diameter and are coloured dark green or black. We make the handle about 375mm (15 inches) long. If a light coloured net is used, the birds will avoid it more readily than if it were a dark colour and consequently become more stressed than is necessary. Once the bird is in the net, place your hand over the bird's shoulders with the forefinger against the neck, just below the skull. Place your thumb on the opposite side of the neck and gently apply a slight upward pressure to the base of the skull. This prevents the bird from manoeuvring into a biting position and you can control the bird quite easily. Practice with a budgerigar or smaller parrot will soon familiarise you with handling, minimising damage to your fingers or the bird.

The use of a heavy glove should be avoided, as the feeling of the hand is lost and severe damage can be incurred to the bird if too much pressure is applied.

Carry Box

After many years of transporting birds, over long distances by road and from aviary to aviary in our own yard, we have found it essential to use a good style of carry box that is comfortable and less stressful for the occupants on these journeys.

No doubt, we have all seen different types of carry boxes made of various materials. Boxes that are too large or of all wire construction are totally unsuitable, as the bird does not feel secure and will probably injure itself before reaching its destination. Also, people that purchase and collect birds using dirty or poorly constructed carry boxes, give the impression that this is how they look after and house their birds.

1. The type of box we use.
2. Unsuitable and dirty cage and carry box.
3. Held back to back in one hand.
4. Birds ready for surgical sexing.

Since we began surgically sexing our birds, we found it necessary to use a carry box of uniform size that stacks easily, as up to 30 birds at a time are individually boxed and numbered with the minimum of fuss and with no mix-ups once sexing is completed.

The carry box we have designed works extremely well. It is made of 9mm (3/8 inch) plyboard, 400mm (15.7 inches) long x 230mm (9 inches) wide x 230mm (9 inches) high with a false roof angled in the top, similar to a budgerigar show cage.

A 65mm (2.5 inch) diameter hole is cut in the actual top, 65mm (2.5 inches) from the back of the box, so as two boxes can be carried back to back in each hand. Without a conventional style handle screwed on the top, the boxes can stack on top of one another and air can flow through the hole to the box behind with no fear of suffocation, plus the box behind is in semi-dark keeping the occupants dark and less stressed.

In one end, a hole cut with a large hole or jig saw 120mm (4.7 inches) in diameter, large enough to get your hand through without skinning your knuckles, enables retrieval of the bird without applying too much pressure.

This cut out centre piece is retained and used for the door, affixed with a 50mm (2 inch) hinge. A good quality pad bolt screwed on in a vertical position will reduce the chances of the door accidentally opening through vibration.

We have all had first hand experience or know of someone that has been in the embarrassing situation of birds loose in the rear of the vehicle, or worse still, just an empty box on reaching one's destination.

For the front of the carry box, a frame is made of 25mm (1 inch) 18 gauge angle for the two sides and top, with 50mm (2 inches) being used for the bottom to prevent seed falling out.

25mm x 12.5mm (1 inch x 1/2 inch) weldmesh is pop rivetted to the inside of this frame which then fits neatly on the front, held in position with a wood screw in each corner.

We find a front such as described, is far easier than mesh that is attached permanently. It is simple to remove for cleaning or repainting as required.

Boxes are painted with a water-based paint (Wattle Guard™ Low Sheen Pinewood Green) which is a dull colour and the mesh fronts are painted with a Gold colour metal primer. Any colour can be used. We just prefer these colours.

A few sheets of newspapers placed on the floor will enable the bird to grip, preventing slipping, this being replaced when soiled. We strictly adhere to one bird per box. This eliminates squabbling or fighting etc.

Having supplied many of these boxes to fellow aviculturists throughout Australia, they have been used for Lovebird to Eclectus sized parrots with good results.

For despatching stock overseas we use clean plyboard boxes built to suit the species - reasonably low in height with limited viewing area but enough to allow air flow. We prefer to nail the top down with no doors to be opened. Address to the receiver clearly indicating name, phone number and other relevant details, including the senders' address and contact details. If permits are required, these should be attached to the box. Always check with the airlines regarding flight times and advise the receiver at least 24 hours in advance. We have despatched many consignments within Australia and overseas with no problems if these few guidelines are adhered to.

Housing

Building aviaries is something we have done a lot of and after extensive travelling and looking at all types of constructions, we still prefer the open flight type aviary attached to a solid shelter.

All areas are different with regards to location but we prefer aviaries to face east, as the occupants get the morning sun which stimulates activity during the day ahead. We believe the sun is very important in stimulating birds to breed, along with having access to natural rain to maintain feather condition and provide moisture for incubation. Be aware that, Asiatic Parrots do not bathe in the water bowl as many native parrot species do.

Above and below: Parrot breeding flights at the authors' property.

In our area, we experience many cold, damp days with no sun for days on end, therefore we have found it necessary to build the frame of the shelter from hardwood timber and the divisions from cement sheeting. The ceiling is also lined with cement sheeting, helping to insulate against condensation directly off the corrugated iron roof.

We find an insulated shelter is far warmer and maintains a more even temperature than the commercial type aviaries that are manufactured to a price, out of flat iron and pop rivets. They can become either freezing cold or excessively hot.

For the flight section 20mm (3/4 inch) galvanised pipe is used for the frame as this is far stronger than 12mm (1/2 inch) galvanised pipe and one is able to strain the netting on neat and taut without bowing the frames. We prefer to tie wire netting onto galvanised pipe rather than to pop rivet weldmesh onto box steel tubing, although this is totally up to individual choice.

It is getting harder to obtain good quality netting nowadays and the next alternative is to use weldmesh. However, we have found that birds damage their feathers on weldmesh more than they do on netting. For Asiatic Parrots the size of weldmesh selected can vary. The choice should be made with a view to keeping undesirable creatures out (including wild finches) rather than

Above and below:
Parrot breeding flights.

the Asiatics in, so always buy as small as you can afford. Minimum gauge or thickness should be 17 gauge (1.3mm).

A safety passage is necessary in a breeding block of aviaries and we prefer one at the rear, wide enough for wheelbarrow access to be used for cleaning etc. Also, birds fly to the front of the aviary when attending to feeding etc. from the rear. Full height doors also save the back and a lot of head butting.

Roofing one third of the flight section adjacent to the shelter with fibreglass sheeting provides more protection and is an ideal area to hang nest logs or boxes.

In building aviaries, vermin proofing should always be considered and the fewer places for rodents to get established the better. The floors of our shelters are of concrete and the flights earth. If we find evidence of rats or mice, we use poison in bait boxes along with regular digging and hosing of their tunnels. You just have to be as persistent as they are in order to keep their numbers down. As well as being disease carriers, mice attract cats and snakes.

Suspended cages are very popular today, being easy to clean, cheaper to construct than conventional aviaries and housing more breeding pairs in a small area. However, in the short time they have been in use, we have already had reports from America that a lot of larger type parrots (African Greys, Major Mitchell's Cockatoos etc.) reared under these conditions are very poor flyers and feather problems are on the increase. Although Indian Ringnecked Parrots can be bred in such cages, 600-900mm (2-3 feet) wide x 1.8m (6 feet) long x 1.2m (4 feet) high, we would suggest they be housed in

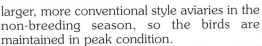

larger, more conventional style aviaries in the non-breeding season, so the birds are maintained in peak condition.

Water is provided by running a 20mm (3/4 inch) galvanised or PVC black irrigation pipe the full length of the breeding complex with a 4.5mm (3/16 inch) hole drilled adjacent to each water bowl. It is then just a matter of turning on the supply tap to fill each water bowl. Bowls must still be regularly scrubbed clean.

To gain maximum flight, perches are provided both in the shelter and at the front of the flight. We use natural black tea-tree branches which when dry are extremely hard and last well, before they need replacing.

Above and right: View into aviary shelter.
Below left: Rear walkway.
Below right: Nest log hung under fibreglass sheeting roof provides more protection.

Cleaning in and around seed dishes takes place weekly, however we have a major clean up after the moult, around March in Australia, when the shelters are cleaned of all seed and feathers, the walls scrubbed and the dirt floors of the flights raked over. At this time, liberal amounts of lime are spread and dug in, helping to sterilise the floor. Birds remain in their flights whilst this is carried out.

'New Wire' Disease

Asiatic Parrots are inquisitive and like to nibble in a new aviary, which predisposes these birds to 'new wire' disease. 'New wire' disease is heavy metal (zinc) poisoning caused by ingestion of the zinc coating on new wire or ingestion of fresh solder joining the wire. It is advisable not to house any birds in a cage or aviary which has not been weathered or 'deactivated' with a thorough wire scrub using vinegar.

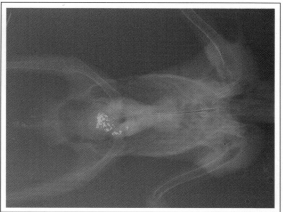

Above: Nest log with removeable inspection door.
Right: A radiograph of a bird that has chewed the galvanised wire on its aviary. The bright white dots in the abdomen are metal particles. This is the best way to diagnose this problem, which is more common than many people realise.
Below: The difference between 'clean' wire and that coated with white zinc oxide powder is quite obvious.

Symptoms of 'new wire' disease will appear within a few days to weeks depending on the amount of 'new wire' ingested. The first symptom may be 'sleepy' eyes, but may quickly develop into vomiting, lethargy followed by paralysis and death.

Veterinary treatment will save most birds suffering from 'new wire' disease, as long as the kidneys have not been irreversibly damaged. Early veterinary attention, therefore, will preserve your investment.

Nesting Logs and Nestboxes

Nest logs, which last longer than nestboxes, are now used in all our aviaries with the larger type parrots, who love to chew. In our early days we used nestboxes of sawn timber or plyboard and one was forever replacing them. There is nothing worse than the bottom falling out or a hole appearing in the side of the nestbox due to the hen chewing away from the inside. This usually happens the day the young hatch and often it is pouring with rain, resulting in the young and the breeding season being lost for another twelve months.

We spend many hours of a night preparing natural hollows for the coming breeding season, making use of natural knot holes and cutting them to various lengths to suit different species. We are sure

much of our breeding successes are attributed to these natural hollows, which is most satisfying. A 380mm (15 inches) strap of 25mm (1 inch) flat iron is bolted to each nest log so that it can be hung securely.

Debates still arise on how logs or boxes should be hung, whether vertically or on an angle. All our logs are hung vertically with very few problems. If you have hens that are clumsy in the nest, breaking or cracking eggs due to entry, we have found they are not worth persevering with as they often don't make good mothers and the offspring are likely to be the same. It is far simpler just to cull the hen and replace with a better bird. It must be stated again that these procedures and suggestions work for us. If your particular methods produce successful results, maintain them.

Of all the types of material available for use in a nesting chamber, we still prefer rotted hardwood sawdust. A supply of this is obtained from a local sawmill and left in the open to decay. Sawdust holds a certain amount of moisture and can be rammed down firmly in the log, not becoming too dusty.

Sawdust is renewed soon after the shortest day (21st June, in Australia), in preparation for the coming breeding season. Regular checks are made up until eggs are laid, checking that the sawdust has not been removed and that stones or other hard objects have not been placed in the log by the birds.

Nest logs are left in the aviary all year round as Asiatic Parrots often use them if disturbed or threatened by hawks and other predators.

Above: Hen Slaty-headed Parrot at the entrance to her nest log.
Right. Typical nest log used by the authors.
Below left: Hen Moustache Parrot on her nest log.
Below right: Inspection doors are a must with heavy logs - young Alexandrines can be seen here.

Feeding

We may be criticised by many breeders for not feeding a greater variety of foodstuffs, however, we just do not have the time to give all the birds sprouted seed, fruit, vegetables, vitamin supplements etc. in the variety and amounts some breeders advocate.

If we were to feed all these additional foods to the amount of birds we keep, it would result in all day being taken up with food preparation and feeding.

We know of birds that have responded well to a smorgasbord type diet and we know of birds that have deteriorated on such a diet. The majority of reports of feeding a rich, varied diet to pairs of birds have indicated little or no improvement in either the breeding pairs or the number or physique of their offspring. Therefore, in our opinion, providing your birds are receiving an adequate, nutritional diet, anything more is of little benefit.

When feeding essential extras, it is important they are supplied on a daily basis. Many problems arise when a particular fruit or vegetable is unavailable or may be of poor quality. This can easily upset your birds. Feed what you have time to prepare and use foods that can be obtained throughout most of the year. If our birds were suffering in any way from a dietary deficiency we would take steps to remedy that situation, however many of our birds have been breeding successfully since the 1960's.

Working in an apple orchard, Syd often observes the feeding habits of wild Rosellas. No attempt will be made to attack the crop until the fruit is fully ripe, when the sugar content is high. Nowadays, for cold storage purposes, we pick fruit before it reaches maturity, hence no wild bird problems. Fruit out of cold storage would not be eaten if it were still on the tree, therefore apart from about eight weeks of the year it would be virtually impossible to obtain apples to the birds liking. Fruit seems to go off quickly and this uneaten fruit must be removed to avoid bacteria problems. Sprouted seed falls into the same category. One infected batch and you may lose all your youngsters for the year. It is not suggested you should not feed sprouted seed to your birds, however, if you do not have the time to prepare these foods properly, to avoid possible risks to the birds' health, do not include them in their diet.

Seed Diet

Our basic seed mix consists of 2 parts grey-striped sunflower, 1 part hulled oats and 1 part budgerigar mix. The budgerigar seed mix consists of 50% plain canary and 50% mixed pannicum, Japanese and French white millet seeds. This is fed once a week, either in self feeders or open dishes on the floor, twelve months of the year. When the birds are moulting, niger and rape seed should form about 2% of the seed mix. We believe that birds regulate their diet, as at certain times of the year it is quite noticeable that some seeds are preferred more than others.

A seed diet alone is insufficient for birds. During breeding and moulting the protein level required by the birds is not met. Many of the essential amino acids that make up proteins are low or non existent. Vitamin content is variable and the mineral content depends on the ground where the seed was grown. The basic seed diet should therefore be supplemented.

Above. Corn cobs and milk thistle hung up on 'S-hook'.
Right:
Corn cobs thawed.

Fruit and Vegetable Supplements

After experimenting with various types of fruit and vegetables, soaked seed and different seeding grasses, we have chosen corn on the cob and milk thistles in flower as an excellent supplement.

We find milk thistles and oats in head (grown on home ground), corn on the cob, some fruit and dry dog food or parrot pellets meets dietary requirements.

Corn cobs are purchased through a wholesale fruiterer, in season, when they are at their best quality and value. We purchase around 10,000 corn cobs a year and it's a family effort removing the outer leaf before taking them to a commercial freezer works where they are snap frozen and stored until required.

Once young start hatching (early September, in Australia), we bring home 1,500 cobs at a time which are held in a small freezer.

We feed about 200 cobs a day in the peak of our breeding season, which are taken out of the freezer the night before and left to thaw out on a stainless steel sink ready for feeding.

Small 'S-hooks' made of 8 gauge (4mm) plain wire are used to hang the cobs in the aviaries allowing the birds to chew completely around the cob. With the kernel attached to the core, birds have to eat through each individual kernel and in doing this, there is minimum waste, except for the core. Some larger parrots often chew the core as well.

Above: Milk thistles. Below: Corn cobs on stainless steel sink, thawing.

Our parrots readily accept sweet corn and seem to prefer cobs that have been frozen and thawed, to fresh cobs. Possibly, the reason for this is that there is often a time gap between the grower and the consumer. With our method, corn cobs are always frozen within 24 hours of picking so they retain their moisture and sweetness.

Usually one cob daily per pair feeding young is sufficient, however, the amount consumed will depend on the number of young being fed. Also, the larger the species the more they consume, eg. an Alexandrine Parrot is going to eat more than a Plum-headed Parrot. The general rule in our complex is if they do not consume what is given, they are fed less the following day.

Once young fledge, corn cobs are one of the first things they eat, so we continue providing them for another four weeks. By then, they

have learnt to crack seed, therefore we discontinue the corn cobs.

Some people feed corn all year round, however, in our situation we would need to buy our own freezer works and employ someone expressly to carry out this chore.

As mentioned earlier, we also use milk thistles in flower. Fortunately, we can still obtain a regular supply of this excellent green food. We prefer to pick thistles in the cool of the morning and have them in the aviaries within the hour. If picked in the heat of the day, the flowers are in full bloom and have released most of their seeds and will soon wilt. Feeding them fresh, stalk, leaf and flower heads are completely consumed. Shell grit and cuttlefish bone are also provided regularly for calcium requirements. This is our basic diet, fed daily. Any other foodstuffs such as fruit or seeding grasses are given on a casual basis - more as treats than anything else. We are very satisfied with the results we have achieved using this simple diet.

It should be noted that there are a great many foods that will be eaten by your birds, but they need only be fed a few of these items providing they supply the balanced diet of vitamins, minerals and proteins the birds require.

Other foods providing vitamins which are beneficial to your birds include:

Vitamins A, D3 and E
Carrots (best boiled for a few minutes to release vitamin A)
Broccoli
Silverbeet (silverbeet contains oxalic acid which prevents the absorption of calcium by the bird. To avoid this problem, silverbeet should be boiled for a few minutes, particularly before being fed to laying hens or young growing birds).
Pawpaw
Watermelon

Vitamin B
Seeding grasses
Sprouted seeds
Dark green vegetables

Vitamin E
Wheatgerm

More protein is necessary for birds that are moulting or breeding. It is suggested that once a week, feed one hard-boiled egg yolk and a cooked chicken leg from the dinner table between a pair of birds. Egg yolk provides animal protein and vitamins A, D, E, K and B. Chicken bone provides animal protein and minerals.

A variety of fruits and vegetables offered daily are beneficial to your birds

Breeding

Keeping Records

To be successful in breeding Asiatic Parrots, or in fact, any form of livestock, one must keep accurate records and conduct a strict culling programme. Otherwise, you will soon find that after a few years your stock will deteriorate. Breeding performances will be poor and it is not long before your collection is just a lot of 'has beens'.

If breeding mutations, young should be closed rung at 8-15 days of age for identification purposes and records kept of parentage. If this is done, stock can be sold and guaranteed to the purchaser with confidence. If not closed rung, all sorts of things can happen, from birds being switched, doors left open and birds becoming mixed up and so the list and excuses go on.

Ringing

Metal split rings that are placed on adult birds often cause problems, as the bird, not being used to having a ring on, naturally tries to remove it and in doing so squeezes the ring tighter, often cutting off circulation possibly resulting in the loss of a leg. There are split rings available, made of stainless steel, that are applied with a special pair of pliers and cannot be squeezed tighter by the bird. Unless it is absolutely necessary, be careful using metal split rings.

Stock Management

Over a period of years, you can improve your stock type and colour by selecting the better birds to breed with. Some people never know a good bird from a bad one. We are always on the look out for better type birds in other collections and are ready to compliment their owners. You must never think you have the best.

In building up a collection, we find that your chances of success are increased if you have at least three or more breeding pairs of a particular species. It is then possible to compare each breeding performance and you are able to select young for replacements from pairs that lay a good size clutch, have a high fertility rate, have good mothering ability and raise young that are true to type with no deformities, as most of these factors are hereditary. It is up to the breeder to take advantage of these characteristics.

Culling should be applied to birds that are poor parents and have small clutches, poor fertility, weak eyesight, crossed wings, turned in feet or are weak bodied birds that sit low on the perch and so on.

Odd coloured feathers are usually the first signs of weakness or deficiencies and should also be avoided. Stock bred out of season should also be discouraged, as they are often weak. Their parents should have bred during the season proper, so out of season birds are often from third clutches. Many are handreared or reared by foster parents, as few Asiatic Parrots regularly double or triple brood. What has to be remembered is that they are hatching from the ninth to fifteenth egg laid by the hen in the one year. Such eggs are usually never as good as the first eggs laid. So these chicks are always off to a bad start in life and usually do not improve.

Always remember that your stock can only respond to the treatment they are given and poor performances are often the fault of the owners.

Pairing and Mating

Pair bonding is another important factor in the successful breeding of any bird. It may take a number of years before some species attempt to nest, however with most Asiatic Parrots, they pair up reasonably easily. Bonding in these species is not as permanent or as strong as in other species of parrots. In breeding Indian Ringnecked Parrot mutations, we have on many occasions broken up pairs for a particular mating with no problems. They settle down with their new partner within weeks and breed successfully.

In Victoria, Asiatic Parrots mainly breed between July and October.

Courtship and mating usually begins three to four weeks before egg laying commences. If you haven't seen Asiatic Parrots displaying, you could be excused for thinking they were having an epileptic fit. With eyes rolling and dilating and the body stretching and bowing while taking short hops on the perch, their performance is quite different to our native species.

Mating usually takes place soon after this display and we have observed them mating on the ground and on top of the nest log, but normally on the perch, not bothering them whether it is swinging or fixed. Mating occurs several times a day from dawn until dusk.

Approximate incubation times are given under the individual species sections in this book. It is difficult to record incubation periods, because although the hen is in the nest log or nestbox, it does not mean she is actually incubating the eggs. After 10-14 days, inspection should be made to see if the eggs are fertile. If eggs are removed for fostering out, incubation, or because they are clear, there is a good likelihood the hen will lay a second clutch. However, once the parents are feeding young there is much less likelihood of a second clutch being laid, even if the young are removed for handrearing.

Pair of Cinnamon Grey-green Indian Ringnecked Parrots.

Handraising
Asiatic Parrots

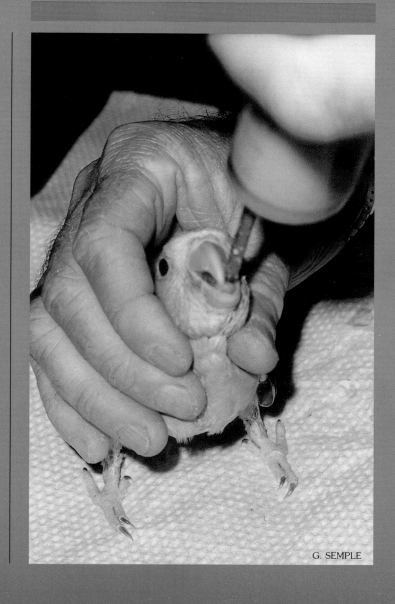

Handraising Asiatic Parrots

This section is a simple guide to aid the reader who may find him or herself in the position of foster parent. The method put forward here is adequate for chicks seven days old or older. Rearing chicks from the egg or from one or two days old is much more complicated. Eggs or very young chicks should be fostered out to the nests of similar species or to Fischer's or Peachfaced Lovebirds until at least a week old, whenever possible.

When the chicks are removed from the nest they should be taken inside and placed in a warm receptacle, such as a thermostatically controlled brooder. This wonderful appliance is fortunately not necessary for Asiatic chicks a week or more of age, especially if there are two, three or more chicks that can huddle together to keep warm. All that is required is a suitable container and a heat source. A cardboard box is quite sufficient, as it retains heat and moisture. The lid can be closed to keep the chicks in the dark as in their natural nest. Boxes, available in various sizes, can be burned when soiled.

Mention the words heat source and many people will think 'light bulb'. Light bulbs do give off heat but they also shed light which can be unpleasant to the chicks. To obtain heat but no illumination from a light bulb is quite a task and can lead to a smoke-filled room or worse. A couple of much simpler methods are (a) sit the box or boxes on an electric blanket (covered with a sheet of cardboard or similar). This can be kept on low heat - especially at night. (b) Take the element out of a warming slipper, wrap it in newspaper and tape secure. Place in the box leaning against one side. The chicks will sit beside it or move away, regulating the amount of heat they require. It will not catch fire. We have been using this method very successfully. Depending on your location or the time of year, artificial heat may not be required at all.

Now that the chicks are comfortably housed leave them alone for a few hours. Having just moved them to a new environment chicks are more inclined to eat well for the first time when they are really hungry. Obviously if the crops are empty and the chicks are starving they should be offered food immediately.

As the chicks feather up and become more recognisable as birds they will not require heat unless it is really cold. They should be placed in a wire cage or the like. A cage without a base sitting on sheets of newspaper is very convenient for cleaning etc.

Handrearing Formula

Although there are some excellent commercial handrearing formulas available, we prefer our own recipe. Ultimately, it is up to the breeder and how much effort one is prepared to put in or has the time to spend.

The following mixture is very simple. The ingredients are readily and conveniently available.

Ingredients

2 parts Heinz™ high protein baby cereal
1 part Uncle Toby's™ rolled oats
1 part sunflower kernels
Powdered cuttlebone
Pentavite™ multi-vitamin liquid - two drops per chick, daily.
Silverbeet water

Method

Dry Mixture

Place the required amount of sunflower kernels in a blender and blend. Add the rolled oats and blend. Add the high protein baby cereal and cuttlefish powder at the rate of two teaspoons per 500 grams of mix.

The baby cereal and cuttlefish powder does not need blending, however the blender makes a good and easy job of thoroughly mixing the ingredients together. Place the mixture in an airtight container until required.

Silverbeet Water

Boil a silverbeet leaf for a few minutes. Place it in the blender with a little water and blend. Finely sieve the liquid into a jug or cup.

Feeding Time

Place the desired amount of dry mixture (trial and error initially), in a cup or small bowl. Add some cold silverbeet water and stir into a thick paste (cold water prevents lumps forming). Add boiling water from the kettle and mix to a yoghurt-like consistency (so it will slowly pour off a teaspoon).

Place the cup in a bowl of boiling water to keep it hot when feeding the birds. Add two drops of Pentavite™ multi vitamin liquid and stir into one meal per day.

A syringe or 'bent' spoon can be used to feed chicks. We find a more natural feeding response is encouraged when the 'beak-like' bent spoon is used. Place a spoon on its side in a vice or similar and tighten down until the sides of the spoon bend in.

Lift one chick out of the box and place it on a towel or sponge so it cannot slide about. Place one hand over the bird's back supporting its head, between thumb and forefinger. Test the temperature of the

Crop feeding a Plum-headed Parrot.

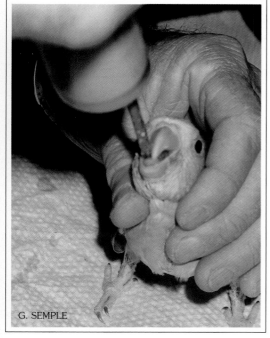

G. SEMPLE

food against your top lip. It should be very warm but not scalding. Place the end of the spoon under the tip of the chick's top mandible and gently raise the spoon and pour the food into its mouth. Chicks take to the spoon very quickly and feeding will soon present no problems. Chicks should be fed one at a time. Three chicks fighting over a food laden spoon becomes very messy. If the chick refuses to eat, it is usually because the food is not warm enough. After feeding, wipe any excess food from the chick's face or throat. After a feed the crops should be seen to be full, but not bloated. The chicks should be fed when their crops are 90% empty. This will be approximately 3-5 feeds per 24 hours, depending on the age. The first feed will be first thing in the morning, the last feed just before one goes to bed. As the birds get older the food mixture can be made thicker and feeds less frequent. Gradually, supply canary seed, sunflower kernels, sprouted mung beans, some egg and biscuit mix, placed on paper under the cage or in shallow bowls or trays. The chicks will start pecking at this food within a few days,

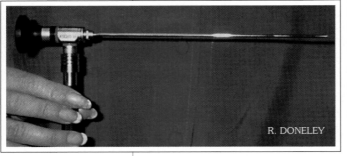

Above: Syringe and bent spoon.
Below: Endoscope - used for surgical sexing.

R. DONELEY

gradually refusing spoon feeds. Soon, in the mornings, hard seeds can be felt in their crops. There is really no problem in weaning birds. The birds will do it by themselves.

Surgical Sexing

This is a safe procedure performed under a gas anaesthetic which allows birds to be sexed at a young age, giving the aviculturist the opportunity to select definite pairs before the breeding season. This is most beneficial with this expensive group of birds. It requires an avian veterinarian to perform the procedure. A very small fibre optic light (endoscope) is inserted into the abdominal cavity through a small incision and the sex organs are visualised.

Asiatic Parrots take from two to three years to reach sexual maturity. The surgical sexing procedure is most reliable in birds older than six months of age. The procedure is sometimes inconclusive in birds younger than six months, because the sex organs have not become large enough to identify positively.

During the procedure other organs are examined for abnormalities and the bird's breeding capability can also be determined.

Sickness

No matter how small your involvement in bird keeping, attempts should be made to broaden your knowledge on how to recognise and treat a sick bird. Inspect each aviary daily, to maintain early detection of problems.

Within 24 hours a bird can deteriorate very quickly and if you only check your birds weekly, it is often too late to rectify a problem. Birds can suffer from stress - from just being moved from one aviary to another, night frights caused by cats or owls, bright car lights, sudden changes in temperature, to name a few.

If birds are off-colour, they usually fluff up and generally look listless. If showing these signs and sitting on two legs, they are not well. Birds perching on one leg are usually just resting.

In our safety corridors, a small hole is drilled through the wall so as to observe the birds without disturbing them. This way you will soon recognise if they are off-colour. It is important to remember that if you find a sick bird, the quicker you take action the better the chances of its recovery.

Diseases of
Asiatic Parrots

R. DONELEY

*Alexandrine
Parrot with
spinal
deformity.*

Diseases of Asiatic Parrots

Introduction

The Asiatic Parrot family are generally more resistant to diseases compared to Australian species of parrots. However, this does not mean these birds are totally immune to disease. Poor management practices or exposure to highly virulent diseases will cause serious illness and even death, in all species, including the Asiatic.

Common Health Problems in Asiatic Parrots

The Asiatic species have problems with bacterial bowel infections. The first sign of illness is diarrhoea followed by lethargy. This can be seen in birds fed contaminated sprouted seed, however is more likely due to worm infestation. The treatment is to stop feeding sprouted seed and a short course of antibiotics.

Alexandrine and Indian Ringnecked Parrots appear to be prone to acute infections of Aspergillosis. The *Aspergillus* fungus is usually associated with fruit and vegetables left in the aviary for longer than twelve hours. Wet areas and condensation in the aviary will also be predisposed to Aspergillosis. Aspergillosis may be seen in a sudden onset of severe respiratory distress (gaping and open mouth breathing) in Asiatics. A cure is rarely successful without surgery. Therefore, early veterinary attention will help these birds.

Chlamydiosis (Psittacosis) is a disease seen in neglected Indian Ringnecked and Plum-headed Parrots. The birds may have been housed in a large aviary with other species of birds. The birds often have other diseases at the same time but the cause of the illness is usually due to the highly toxic *Chlamydia* organism.

Other problems of note in Asiatic Parrots include worm infestations, Papovavirus, bite wounds (especially toe injuries), Megabacteria, nestling viral disease and rickets in young.

Prevention and Control of Disease within the Aviary

Good management prevents disease within the aviary. Good management takes into account the system of housing and quarantine, aviary hygiene, breeding preferences, proper nutrition, accurate record keeping and an informed policy against disease. By providing the best physical and psychological environment for captive birds, breeding results are maximised and disease minimised.

Stress and Disease

Stress makes birds more susceptible to disease. Slaty-headed and Plum-headed Parrots are particularly susceptible to stress. Stress can be brought on from noise, from dogs and cats or from other predators such as rats and mice, an incorrectly designed aviary, unhygienic aviary management, incorrect diet during the breeding season or occurrences which affect the physical and psychological well-being of the bird. Stress control is an important part of disease prevention.

Basic Rules used to Prevent Disease entering an Aviary

- Only purchase healthy and alert birds.
- Do not purchase birds in poor feather or with tail feathers missing, with watery eyes, or 'going light'.
- Quarantine all newly purchased birds for six to eight weeks in an isolation cage and treat for worms.
- Observe for illness whilst in quarantine.

- Ill birds in quarantine must be diagnosed and treated appropriately before entering the main aviary.
- Only healthy quarantined birds are to enter your main aviary.

Recognising Disease

Early recognition of disease is extremely important if these diseases are to be controlled. Because birds have the ability to hide their illnesses, known as the Preservation Reflex, any bird that appears sick must be helped immediately.

Good aviary management must include a proper surveillance of the flock for signs of illness. With careful observation these signs will become very clear and alert you to take immediate first aid steps. It is best to observe the birds from a distance before closer observation of the flock. This way it is possible to see how the birds are behaving in their undisturbed environment, also any abnormal behaviour can be more accurately determined.

Signs of illness vary according to the disease involved, but initially there are some general changes which occur in the behavioural pattern and physical appearance of an ill bird.

Observe whether your bird is less active than normal, fluffed up with both feet on the perch, rubbing its head on the perch, has a slight tail bob, has its head behind its wing, is sitting low on the perch, appears sleepy, is not eating with the other birds, does not fly away when you enter the cage, or is lethargic on the ground.

The bird may also sneeze, display wet feathers around the head, a wet eye, a shut eye, a droopy wing, faeces stuck to the vent or tail feathers, or be unable to fly.

Once recognised as being ill, the bird should be moved to a specially designed hospital cage which should be away from the aviary. This cage provides an opportunity for the bird to rest in a controlled environment, isolates the bird from other birds and allows you to more closely observe the bird and to implement any intensive treatment which may be necessary.

Health Check of Newly Acquired Birds

The most important aspect in maintaining the health of Asiatic Parrots is to acquire a bird already in good health. The emphasis here is the health of the new bird (rather than the risk of disease entering your aviary), because most Asiatic Parrots represent quite a sizeable investment for any aviculturist. This investment is best protected by a complete physical examination before purchase and a health check after purchase (with the full knowledge of the vendor). The health check should be done by an avian veterinarian. This diagnosis will indicate any diseases which may affect the long term livelihood and breeding capabilities of the new purchase. Other less serious diseases may also be detected and appropriate therapy can be dispensed at this time to prevent future problems. A bird diagnosed as having a serious disease which cannot be cured with appropriate medication or which will affect the breeding capabilities of the bird, should not be purchased.

Nowadays, with the modern day diagnostic procedures available it is possible to buy a bird and guarantee its health at the time of purchase.

The health check benefits all aviculture by:
- Providing a means of a guarantee of an expensive bird.
- Removes the responsibility from the vendor to the buyer after a health check is completed satisfactorily.

- Discourages the unscrupulous sale of unfit birds to the unsuspecting aviculturist.

Physical Examination

A complete physical examination of the newly acquired bird is necessary if a health check by an avian veterinarian is not performed. The most important part of the examination is to handle the bird. A careful examination begins at the head, checking the eyes, the nostrils, the feathers around the nostrils, the head, body, wings and especially the tail for signs of abnormal feathers, the vent for signs of pasting and the keel bone for 'going light'. The bird must be checked carefully for watery eyes and discoloured or malformed nostrils. These are signs of conjunctivitis and sinusitis. Left untreated for any period of time, these diseases often become impossible to cure. Both are symptoms of Chlamydiosis (Psittacosis) or a bacterial infection. Chlamydiosis is a particularly dangerous disease to humans as well as birds and you must be able to recognise its symptoms. A bird which has a prominent keel bone is said to be 'going light'. This has many causes, most of which are dangerous to your resident flock. Such a bird should not be purchased. It is very important to check the feathers. Many feather abnormalities seen in this group of birds indicate virus diseases such as Papovavirus or Psittacine Beak and Feather Disease (PBFD). The physical check of the new bird is the first step in preventing disease from entering your aviaries.

Quarantine of New Birds

The quarantine procedure is necessary to detect any diseased birds which passed the new bird physical check. Some birds appear healthy but in fact may carry a disease. These birds are called 'carriers' and the quarantine procedure allows us to detect such birds. Many of these diseases are stress related and within the six to eight week quarantine period most of these diseases will become apparent. The quarantine procedure is still recommended even with a veterinarian health check.

Quarantine also gives the birds time to acclimatise to their new surroundings so that by the time they enter the aviary they are not in a stress situation. This lessens the chance of introducing disease to your aviary. It is important to place the birds into a quiet, secure quarantine aviary during the day and not at dusk, so as to minimise the chance of wall crashing. It is also necessary to have a quarantine aviary with double wire to prevent aggression between aviary cages. Fighting in the quarantine aviary will stress the birds and make them prone to illness. The quarantine aviary should be away from the main aviary and should provide the new birds with a quiet and secure environment during their acclimatisation. It is best to have birds of the same or compatible species and from the same breeder in the quarantine aviary at the one time, so as to minimise the chance of spreading disease. It is important to carefully observe the new birds for signs of illness, especially signs of loose droppings and watery eyes. Any bird showing signs of illness must be immediately isolated. During the quarantine period Asiatic Parrots should be treated routinely for worms and mites. All healthy quarantined birds are allowed to enter the main aviary after six to eight weeks. It is best to do this on a warm sunny morning so that the birds can adjust easily to the new aviary. The quarantine aviary is then disinfected and cleaned in preparation for the next new purchase.

Quarantine helps in preventing the entry of most disease but it can never be 100% effective. Refer to an avian veterinarian for further advice.

Worm Infestation

Asiatic Parrots spend some time on the ground in captivity and therefore are exposed to infestation of worms from exposed droppings. The most common worms in Asiatic species are Roundworm (*Ascaridia*) and Hairworm (*Capillaria*), although they sometimes can become infested with Tapeworms (*Acuaria*).

Worm Treatment

Treatment of the whole flock is recommended four weeks before and immediately after the breeding season. Wet, humid weather favours an outbreak of Roundworms and if there has been previous problems with worms in the aviary, repeat dosing after such weather conditions.

Another source of infection are wild bird visitors which can leave infective droppings in the aviary. It is important to prevent such visits by sparrows, doves etc. since Roundworms are not species specific. Remember to repeat treatment 14 days later to kill any immature worms which may have escaped the initial treatment.

If worm infestation has been diagnosed, all birds must be treated at the same time with an anthelmintic (anti-worm medicine) which is active against the particular worm and safe to the species of bird. The ideal anthelmintic is one which acts not only on the adult worm but also on the eggs and larvae. Any introduced birds must be treated for worms before entry into the main aviary. This is best done whilst in quarantine.

Regular microscopic testing can identify an unknown source of infestation.

Treatment may affect a clinical cure but ultimate control rests with management. Safe and effective anthelmintics are available. Administration by drinking water gives disappointing results, therefore gavages (medication by crop needle) is more effective.

The most useful method of dosing Asiatic Parrots is by crop needle (size 14). The advantages over in-water medication are that the exact dose can be administered, efficiently and with minimal stress to the bird. Also, Asiatic Parrots drink very little water which again makes crop needle medication necessary. The disadvantages are that the birds must be caught and medicated individually, which is time consuming and can be stressful to the birds.

The size of the crop dictates the volume of mixture or medication that can be given. The adult bird has a much smaller capacity than the nestling. The crop capacity of the adult Plum-headed Parrot is about 2ml and the adult Alexandrine is about 8mls, whereas a baby Indian Ringneck can take 10-20mls of food. The maximum volume to be instilled into the crop of the adult Slaty-headed Parrot is 2mls. If too much volume is given, the medication may enter the lungs and cause pneumonia and death.

Confidence in crop needle use is gained with practice and proper tuition. All avicultural clubs should demonstrate this technique to their members. A good practice is to use sterile water until your technique is polished. Sterile water will not cause pneumonia if only a small amount enters the lung.

Worming Dose Rates

Species	Average Weight	Name and Volume of Anthelminthic		
		Levamisole 0.1ml/l00gm Nilverm™ Pig and Poultry Wormer 16mg/ml	Fenbendazole 0.2ml/100gm Panacur 25™ 25mg/ml for 3 days	Pyrantel 50mg/ml Combantrim™ dilute 1:10 with water 0.2ml/100gm
Alexandrine Parrot	230-240g	0.25ml	0.5ml	0.5ml
Derbyan Parrot	265-270g	0.3ml	0.5ml	0.5ml
Moustached Parrot	125-130g	0.15ml	0.25ml	0.25ml
Indian Ringnecked Parrot	130-140g	0.15ml	0.3ml	0.3ml
Malabar Parrot	80-90g	0.1ml	0.2ml	0.2ml
Plum-headed and Blossum-headed Parrots	70-80g	0.08ml	0. 15ml	0. 15ml
Slaty-headed and Malayan Long-tailed Parrots	90-120g	0.lml	0.2ml	0.2ml

All above dose rates are administered orally with a crop needle.

Ivermectins are now available in many different formulations and strengths. Each formula has a different dose rate so the reader should confer with their avian veterinarian.

Some formulas can be used effectively as spot-on treatments, all are unstable in water and are unreliable given this way. Ivermectins are excellent for the control of mites.

Oxfendazole has gained popularity as an in-water treatment for worms because it has no taste. However, relying on Asiatic Parrots to consume enough water possibly explains why some breeders experience worm problems with their birds. Once again different formulas have differing concentrations. If being administered by crop needle, repeat for three consecutive days.

Fenbendazole should be administered for three consecutive days to ensure effectiveness. This makes it either difficult or unreliable as it cannot be used in water.

Fenbendazole and oxfendazole should not be used during moulting as they may cause feather abnormalities.

Pyrantel is a common ingredient in dog and human wormers and is very effective against nematodes. See table for dose rates. Must be administered by crop needle.

Levamisole is a good old reliable. It has a bitter taste in water, however is very effective administered via crop needle - see dose rates.

DISCLAIMER

Note Carefully: There have been little or no scientific studies documenting the safe use of these anthelmintics (worming medications) in Asiatic Parrots. The use of these drugs remains the full responsibility of the owner of the birds.

The recommended dose rates above have been found to be effective and safe in non-scientific field trials. It is important not to give any other drugs whilst using the above anthelmintics. If there are adverse effects contact your avian veterinarian for advice.

How to Get the Best Out of Your Avian Veterinarian

The bird patient is unique in medical science. No other animal masks the signs of illness so well. It is thought that birds try to hide symptoms of disease due to their natural fear of being attacked by members of their own flock, since the flock does not want any member attracting predators.

This is referred to as the Preservation Reflex. It is this innate ability to hide the signs of illness which makes the job of the avian veterinarian so challenging.

A quick and accurate diagnosis is essential if the bird patient is to be saved. The diagnosis of most bird conditions can be made more quickly now that there are reliable diagnostic procedures available (e.g. blood tests, bacterial culture and special stains used on body fluids). However, an accurate diagnosis can be made difficult, if incorrect first aid treatment is given before the veterinarian is consulted.

Follow the guidelines below before consultation:

The flock-health takes precedence over the health of the individual in the aviary situation and sometimes, sad as it may seem, it becomes necessary to sacrifice the life of one ill bird in order to save the rest of the flock.

• **First assess your disease situation**

If one or at the most two birds fall ill then it is more than likely that there is no serious threat to your aviary. Immediately isolate these ill birds and treat them with appropriate first aid (refer to first aid treatment on next page). Contact your avian veterinarian for further advice. It is important to observe the flock carefully over the following two to five days and if further illnesses occur, then it is almost certain you have an infectious problem. Ill birds should be submitted as soon as possible to the veterinarian for immediate analysis.

• **Submit appropriate birds to the avian veterinarian**

To expedite the correct diagnosis it is imperative that ill or dead birds submitted for analysis have not been treated with any medication. Most tests for bacterial infections will be erroneous if medications are given within 48 hours of testing.

Place clean newspaper or Gladwrap™ on the floor of the transport cage of the ill bird so that droppings can be collected and tested immediately on arrival at the veterinary hospital.

It is best to submit an ill live bird to the veterinarian so that he/she can observe the symptoms and conduct tests on the live bird. Some diseases are difficult to detect in the dead bird and it may be necessary to examine body fluids from the live bird for accurate diagnosis.

Autopsy cannot help in making a correct diagnosis if the bird has been dead for more than six hours. Birds deteriorate very quickly after death and it is important to preserve them as soon after death as possible.

The dead bird must be cooled if the organs are to be preserved for autopsy. This is best achieved by wetting the bird in detergent (to stop the feathers from insulating the body), wrapping the body in paper and then plastic and refrigerating until the body can be taken to the veterinarian. The body is best stored in the vegetable crisper section of the refridgerator if you are able to get to the veterinarian within four days. Longer than this time, then it is best to place it in the freezer section. Transport the body to the veterinarian in a cooler.

A detailed autopsy is sometimes the only way of diagnosing a disease in the aviary. Only a few conditions can be accurately diagnosed at autopsy by looking at the organs alone and it is for this reason that a detailed autopsy is usually required for the exact diagnosis. A detailed autopsy involves taking tests of the body fluids which will give an immediate recommendation for further first aid treatment. For the exact treatment recommendations the organs must be sent to an avian pathologist for microscopic analysis.

• **Immediate first aid treatment which will not delay an accurate diagnosis**

When the bird patient shows signs of illness, the situation must be treated as an emergency. The ill bird's temperature drops rapidly once it stops eating and together with dehydration sends the bird into circulatory failure and kidney shutdown. It is for these reasons that immediate first aid treatment (which will not interfere with the diagnostic testing procedures) should be administered.

1. Isolate an ill bird from healthy birds.
2. Provide warmth and quiet. Keep the temperature within the cage 28° to 30°C (82-86°F). This can be accomplished with a heat lamp placed a few feet from the bird's cage or there are special hospital cages available. In either case check the temperature regularly by observing the bird. If it is still fluffed up, the temperature must be increased and if it is holding the wings out or panting, it is obviously too hot and the temperature must be decreased.
3. Provide food and water. Keep food and water in easy reach.
   Move the food and rearrange the perches so that the food is constantly in front of the bird. Without food, the ill bird's body temperature drops rapidly and without water, dehydration occurs. It is a good idea to learn a force feeding technique utilising a crop needle. A good energy mix for the ill bird is glucose and water (l/4 teaspoon of Glucodin™ powder to 30 mls of water) given warm by crop needle or placed in the water dish. This solution must be made fresh and replaced within twelve hours.
4. Do not give any medication such as antibiotics which may interfere with the diagnostic tests.

Conclusion

This section is a relatively brief overview of diseases and preventative measures to ensure the optimum health of your birds. It is strongly suggested, however, that Dr Mike Cannon's excellent title, **A Guide to Basic Health and Disease in Birds** be read and thoroughly absorbed. This title should certainly be part of any responsible aviculturist's essential reference library.

If in any doubt as to the correct procedure in the treatment of any sick bird, a qualified avian veterinarian should be consulted immediately.

Asiatic Parrot Species

Turquoise Lacewing
Indian Ringnecked
hen.

Above:
Normal green Indian
Ringnecked hen.

Right:
Normal green Indian
Ringnecked cock.

INDIAN RINGNECKED PARROT
Psittacula krameri manillensis

Of the many species of parrots available to aviculture in Australia, the Indian Ringnecked Parrot is one of the most popular birds represented in parrot collections, certainly the most common of the foreign parrots. They have proved to be extremely hardy and reliable breeders.

Looking back over some 30 years of keeping this species, there are not many parrots that we could compare with this lovely Asiatic species. Whether the climate be dry, wet, hot or cold it does not seem to affect their breeding performance. We have seen them housed under all types of conditions, from dark dingy aviaries to large spacious cages completely open with no protection from the weather, but they always battle on. Certainly a lot of our native birds would not last long if they were housed under similar conditions.

Sexing

As with most Asiatic species, the Indian Ringnecked Parrot is extremely difficult to sex under $2-2^1/_2$ years of age, unless surgically sexed. Otherwise, it is a waiting game until black and pink feathers begin to appear, forming a ring around the neck of the cock. The hen remains completely green showing just an indentation where the neck ring should be. Adult plumage is attained at three years of age.

The Indian Ringnecked Parrot looks its worst when moulting and if you are not familiar with this process, you would possibly wonder if something was dramatically wrong with its feathers. Within days, tail feathers drop and pin feathers appear everywhere and the bird looks a total wreck. However, within a few weeks, new feathers replace the old and they are back to their immaculate condition. It is surprising how quickly the cock colours during this moulting period. One week no colour, then completely coloured the next.

Housing

Single pairs should be housed in open flights, one third being covered, varying in overall length from 4.8 metres to 6.6 metres (16 feet to 22 feet). However, experience has proved 4.8 metres (16 feet) in length is generally ample. We have found that the longer the flight, the more speed youngsters get up when first leaving the nest. A branch of leaves or similar placed at each end of the flight prevents damage to heads or wings, on contact with the end wire. Youngsters soon learn the limits of the flight and thereafter there is no problem.

Feeding

Diet includes a basic seed mix of 2 parts grey-striped sunflower, 1 part budgerigar mix, 1 part hulled oats. Boiled corn or corn on the cob are fed when young are in the nest, this being continued until they lose interest in feeding on it, usually about two months after fledging.

Green food is provided daily with milk thistle and/or oats in head being completely consumed, stalk and all.

They seem to eat a variety of foods from seeds, most fruit and vegetables and will be the first to try such commercial products as dry dog food or parrot pellets. We believe they would find food and survive where most other birds would starve.

Breeding

This species is very easy to breed and people who have difficulty, in our opinion, either do not have a true pair, or are simply not trying. Even if nest logs are not provided during the breeding season, we have seen hens digging holes in the earth floor in a desperate bid to form a nesting chamber.

Being such free breeders and long lived birds, one would wonder why they have not saturated their own market. However, having raised over 800 birds in the last 30 years, we find there is still a strong demand for them, especially the mutations.

The 420mm (16.5 inches) long Normal green cock Indian Ringnecked Parrot is a most handsome bird, especially when displaying to his hen, stretching and bowing with eyes dilating. Noises like motor vehicles, lawn mowers etc. passing the aviary usually sets the cock off into a display and with uncoloured birds this is often a guide to their sex. Only the cock displays.

Hollow logs, hung vertically, are used for nesting. These measure 900mm (3 feet) long with an inside diameter of 200-250mm (8-10 inches) with an entrance hole, 75mm (3 inches) in diameter, 150mm (6 inches) from the top. An inspection opening is made 230mm (9 inches) from the bottom. These inspection openings are certainly a timesaver as regular checks can be made on incubating progress and it is easy to remove young birds to be closed rung without removing the log from the wall. Nestboxes should be about 230mm (9 inches) square x 600mm (2 feet) high with a 75mm (3 inches) diameter entrance hole.

Four eggs is a normal clutch, however, five is not unusual. Incubation lasts 21-24 days and the young spend approximately seven weeks in the nest before fledging.

Indian Ringnecked Parrots are excellent parents, rarely letting young die. Many years ago, we had an experience with a Normal pair of Indian Ringnecks. A few days after hatching, a swarm of bees tried to take over the nest log but the parents defended their territory and after a few cans of fly spray and many stings to ourselves, rearing continued with no ill effects.

Albino Indian Ringnecked hen in nesting log with day old young.

1. Indian Ringnecked Parrot eggs.
2. Indian Ringnecked chicks
   approximately four days old.
   (Note the red eye of Lutino chick).
3. Indian Ringnecked chicks
   approximately ten days old
   (Note three Lutinos).
4. Indian Ringnecked chicks
   approximately sixteen days old.

1. Indian Ringnecked chicks
   approximately five weeks old.
2. Lutino, Blue, Green and Albino
   Indian Ringnecked chicks.
3. Blue Indian Ringnecked
   fledglings.

On fledging, the young are often as large in the body as their parents, with a shorter tail. Within a few months it is hard to distinguish them from the adult hen.

Mutations and
Colour Breeding

*Lutino Indian
Ringnecked cock.*

A large attraction in keeping Indian Ringnecked Parrots is the variety of mutations that are available to aviculturists today. Many people are against the establishment of mutations basically on the argument that the offspring are degrading the original species. We can agree with such statements when many so-called mutations often have problems such as: poor eyesight, poor feathering, slow breeding performance and poor colour. Sometimes one either needs a wild imagination to see the colour difference or they are just poor specimens, being of no value to aviculture. On the other hand, there are some excellent mutations that have proved themselves worthy and are well established in collections with Lutino and Blue Indian Ringnecked Parrots being the most popular.

Lutino

In the late 1950's, we had the privilege of viewing the vast parrot collection of Edward Hallstrom of Sydney, which included many species of Macaws, African Greys, Lories, Eclectus etc. But of all these exotic parrots, the birds that appealed to us most were a large colony of Lutino Indian Ringnecked Parrots. These birds were completely yellow, brighter on the face and wing margins with

Blue Indian Ringnecked cock.

the neck ring of the cock being pink and white instead of pink and black as in the Normal bird. This was a sight we will always remember. Soon after that visit we were able to obtain some adult pairs of these magnificent birds which formed the nucleus of our breeding foundation stock. Prior to that, most Lutino mutations in private collections were very poor quality and much work was needed to improve this mutation.

Being sex-linked, it was a slow process to produce split cocks through Normal green hens. Through a strict culling programme over the years we are proud to say that today, Lutinos are as strong as the Normals and are an excellent mutation, praised and admired by many overseas visitors.

Blue

Blue Indian Ringnecked Parrot mutations are off to a better start than Lutinos, simply because they are recessive and the strength is retained, as you are able to produce splits in both cocks and hens from a Normal.

The late Mr Joe Mattinson of Wollongong spent some 20 years developing a blue strain but unfortunately all his birds were disposed of after his death. It is amazing how quickly a collection can be broken up and if we are not careful, within a few years a species can be lost from aviculture forever. However, with careful management and providing accurate records are kept, aviculturists who have Blue mutations should be able to increase the numbers of this beautiful mutation. We both agree that the Blue mutation is as attractive as the Lutino, with the complete body colour being a soft powder blue, brighter on the face, with the cock's neck ring black and white. It may be an illusion or perhaps just the contrast with the blue face, but their red beaks seem to be brighter, as if lacquered, indeed a very handsome bird.

Grey

The Grey Indian Ringnecked Parrot mutation is also a very striking bird. The three tone colours of silver, grey and black make this mutation look very distinguished. The beak is red. The Grey mutation was first bred in Australia by Mr Ian Adcock of New South Wales, and is a dominant mutation.

Grey Indian Ringnecked Parrots are blue series birds. All single factor Grey birds can produce Blue when paired to Blue, Green split Blue or Albino. As most Grey-green birds are bred from Greys, they are split Blue but Grey-green mated to a Green or Grey-green will produce pure Grey-green.

1. Blue Indian Ringnecked hen.
2. Grey Indian Ringnecked cock.
3. Grey Indian Ringnecked hen.

Above:
Albino hen.
Right:
Cinnamon Blue or Skyblue hen.
Below left:
Cinnamon Grey or Silver cock.
Below right: Cinnamon Grey or
Silver hen.

Above left:
Cinnamon Indian
Ringnecked cock.
Above right:
Cinnamon Blue
Indian Ringnecked
hen.

Albino

The Albino mutation is well established in Australia having been bred through Blue and Lutino mutations. These birds are pure white which offsets their red beaks and red eyes in a most striking way. Unlike mammals, it is impossible to produce a single gene albino. The lutino in parrots is the mammalian albino. Therefore in parrots it is correct to call Lutino Blue, Albino. All Albino parrots are Lutino Blue combinations. It is the nature of the pigments.

Cinnamon

Cinnamon is a sex-linked mutation that behaves in the same way as Lutino. If Cinnamon is substituted for Lutino in the following tables on pages 53-56, the expectations are the same except that Lutino becomes Cinnamon and Albino becomes Cinnamon Blue or Skyblue.

Below left:
Cinnamon Grey-green
hen.
Below right:
Cinnamon Grey-green
cock.

Grey-green hen.

Grey-green

When Grey is paired with a Normal green Indian Ringneck (the original dominant colour), progeny produced are Grey-green. This bird is a khaki green colour with black flight and tail feathers. Although in appearance this bird is khaki green or olive in colour, it is called Grey-green because when combined with Blue, produces Grey.

If the dominant grey gene is introduced to Green, the colouring of the young can be Grey-green; to Blue the colouring can be Grey; to Cinnamon the colouring can be Cinnamon Grey-green.

It must be understood that a hen cannot be split for a sex-linked mutation and the dominant Grey-green mutation cannot be carried as a split.

However, the lutino and albino colours are not visibly affected by this mutation and any bird carrying it is known as 'masking Grey-green'.

Grey-green cock.

Clearheaded - cleartailed

The Yellowheaded and Whiteheaded mutations now appearing are described in many different head shades, each breeder giving a name according to his own interpretation. Perhaps 'Clearheaded' would be a general description for these mutations. At least three Clearheaded mutations exist, all different genetically, and should not be mixed

Through importation, these Clearheaded-cleartailed birds are now available and we have seen some absolutely stunning examples of what can be produced from this beautiful mutation.

The first Clearheaded mutation appeared in Europe in the early 1980s, a washed out green coloured hen with a bright yellow head. Paired to a Lutino cock, the hen chicks were Lutino and the cock chicks were all Yellowheaded, the same as the mother. This mutation is now called Lacewing. The name Lacewing has been given to a sex-linked Clearheaded bird and is genetically equivalent to a Platinum Cockatiel, rather than a Lacewing Budgerigar. From those beginnings it has been possible to breed different head colours on the many mutations already established.

Yellowheaded Cinnamon and Lacewing are separate mutations in Europe, and a bird cannot be both. The word cinnamon in Yellowheaded Cinnamon has nothing to do with the cinnamon mutation.

In the coming years we will have the opportunity to specialise in whatever colour one desires.

Base colours such as Green, Blue, Lutino, Grey-green etc. will always be needed to use with Par Blue, Fallow, Cinnamon, Pied or Clearheaded-cleartailed.

Above: Lacewing hen.

Left: Lacewing hen.

1. Lacewing hen.
2. Turquoise Lacewing hen.
3. Yellowheaded Cinnamon Grey-green cock.
4. Blue Lacewing hen.

1. Blue Lacewing cock.
2. Turquoise Grey cock.
3. Lightheaded immature
   Red-eyed possible Fallow type.
4. Australian Pied cock.

1. *Pied Indian Ringnecked (possibly acquired) cock.*
2. *Pied Indian Ringnecked cock.*
3. *Turquoise Indian Ringnecked hen.*
4. *Creamino Indian Ringnecked hen.*

General Comments on Mutations

Cinnamon, Turquoise and Fallow are the main colours now being used to produce other mutations. By using these three colours we are able to dilute or enhance established colours such as Blue, Lutino, Grey etc.

Breeders should be careful that the colours produced are easily identified and are representative of the colour name given. Colours that breed true will maintain aviary space, variants will not. Caution should also be taken as to the mixing of recessive, sex-linked and dominant genes, as the resulting offspring cannot be guaranteed 100% as to what they will produce.

The different colour names referred to from country to country is a little confusing at present, but in time hopefully uniform names will be used worldwide.

For example, in Australia what we call Turquoise, is Par Blue or Marine in America and Pastel Blue in Europe (the same bird with four different names). Cinnamon in Australia is referred to as Isabel in Europe.

To cover the genetics of all these individual colours at this stage is rather difficult and we would be only guessing. Unless one knows the exact parentage of stock, unexpected colours can appear. Overseas, many colours are still in the experimental stage with varying opinions as to what will be produced.

For example, we mated a Green cock split for Cinnamon and Blue, to a hen Cinnamon Grey-green split Blue and they produced six different colours (Albino, Skyblue, Silver, Ivory, Grey and Cinnamon). We are at a loss as to how an Albino bird appeared out of this mating. Obviously the cock must also have been split for Lutino, but not to our knowledge.

There are certainly some exciting years ahead for Indian Ringnecked Parrot breeders.

From past experience we have found that many people do not want to know about the actual mechanics of genetic inheritance. The expected progeny results of a certain pairing is all they are really interested in. So for all Indian Ringneck mutation breeders, we have listed some matings and their expectations in the following tables starting on page 53.

**Blue cock and
Cinnamon
Grey-green hen**

Mutant Breeding Combinations and Theoretical Expectations of Indian Ringnecked Parrots

Parents	Progeny			
Cock x Hen	%	Cock	%	Hen
Green x Green/Blue	25 25	Green/Blue Green	25 25	Green/Blue Green
Green x Lutino	50	Green/Lutino	50	Green
Green x Lutino/Blue	25 25	Green/Lutino Green/Lutino/Blue	25 25	Green Green/Blue
Green x Blue	50	Green/Blue	50	Green/Blue
Green x Albino	50	Green/Lutino/Blue	50	Green/Blue
Lutino x Green	50	Green/Lutino	50	Lutino
Lutino x Green/Blue	25 25	Green/Lutino Green/Lutino/Blue	25 25	Lutino Lutino/Blue
Lutino x Lutino	50	Lutino	50	Lutino
Lutino x Lutino/Blue	25 25	Lutino Lutino/Blue	25 25	Lutino Lutino/Blue
Lutino x Blue	50	Green/Lutino/Blue	50	Lutino/Blue
Lutino x Albino	50	Lutino/Blue	50	Lutino/Blue
Lutino/Blue x Green	25 25	Green/Lutino Green/Lutino/Blue	25 25	Lutino Lutino/Blue
Lutino/Blue x Green/Blue	12.5 25 12.5	Green/Lutino Green/Lutino/Blue Blue/Lutino	12.5 25 12.5	Lutino Lutino/Blue Albino
Lutino/Blue x Lutino	25 25	Lutino Lutino/Blue	25 25	Lutino Lutino/Blue
Lutino/Blue x Lutino/Blue	12.5 25 12.5	Lutino Lutino/Blue Albino	12.5 25 12.5	Lutino Lutino/Blue Albino
Lutino/Blue x Blue	25 25	Green/Lutino/Blue Blue/Lutino	25 25	Lutino/Blue Albino
Lutino/Blue x Albino	25 25	Lutino/Blue Albino	25 25	Lutino/Blue Albino

Cross	%	Offspring	%	Offspring
Green/Lutino x Green	25	Green	25	Green
	25	Green/Lutino	25	Lutino
Green/Lutino x Green/Blue	12.5	Green	12.5	Green
	12.5	Green/Lutino	12.5	Green/Blue
	12.5	Green/Blue	12.5	Lutino/Blue
	12.5	Green/Blue/Lutino	12.5	Lutino
Green/Lutino x Lutino	25	Green/Lutino	25	Green
	25	Lutino	25	Lutino
Green/Lutino x Lutino/Blue	12.5	Green/Lutino	12.5	Green
	12.5	Green/Blue/Lutino	12.5	Green/Blue
	12.5	Lutino	12.5	Lutino
	12.5	Lutino/Blue	12.5	Lutino/Blue
Green/Lutino x Blue	25	Green/Blue	25	Green/Blue
	25	Green/Blue/Lutino	25	Lutino/Blue
Green/Lutino x Albino	25	Green/Blue/Lutino	25	Green/Blue
	25	Lutino/Blue	25	Lutino/Blue
Blue x Green	50	Green/Blue	50	Green/Blue
Blue x Green/Blue	25	Green/Blue	25	Green/Blue
	25	Blue	25	Blue
Blue x Lutino	50	Green/Blue/Lutino	50	Green/Blue
Blue x Lutino/Blue	25	Green/Blue/Lutino	25	Green/Blue
	25	Blue/Lutino	25	Blue
Blue x Blue	50	Blue	50	Blue
Blue x Albino	50	Blue/Lutino	50	Blue
Blue/Lutino x Green	25	Green/Blue	25	Green/Blue
	25	Green/Blue/Lutino	25	Lutino/Blue
Blue/Lutino x Green/Blue	12.5	Green/Blue	12.5	Green/Blue
	12.5	Green/Blue/Lutino	12.5	Lutino/Blue
	12.5	Blue	12.5	Blue
	12.5	Blue/Lutino	12.5	Albino
Blue/Lutino x Lutino	25	Green/Blue/Lutino	25	Green/Blue
	25	Lutino/Blue	25	Lutino/Blue
Blue/Lutino x Lutino/Blue	12.5	Green/Blue/Lutino	12.5	Green/Blue
	12.5	Lutino/Blue	12.5	Lutino/Blue
	12.5	Blue/Lutino	12.5	Blue
	12.5	Albino	12.5	Albino

Cross				
Blue/Lutino x Blue	25	Blue/Lutino	25	Blue
	25	Blue	25	Albino
Blue/Lutino x Albino	25	Blue/Lutino	25	Blue
	25	Albino	25	Albino
Green/Blue x Green	25	Green	25	Green
	25	Green/Blue	25	Green/Blue
Green/Blue x Green/Blue	12.5	Green	12.5	Green
	25	Green/Blue	25	Green/Blue
	12.5	Blue	12.5	Blue
Green/Blue x Lutino	25	Green/Lutino	25	Green
	25	Green/Blue/Lutino	25	Green/Blue
Green/Blue x Lutino/Blue	12.5	Green/Lutino	12.5	Green
	25	Green/Blue/Lutino	25	Green/Blue
	12.5	Blue/Lutino	12.5	Blue
Green/Blue x Blue	25	Green/Blue	25	Green/Blue
	25	Blue	25	Blue
Green/Blue x Albino	25	Green/Blue/Lutino	25	Green/Blue
	25	Blue/Lutino	25	Blue
Green/Blue/Lutino x Green	12.5	Green	12.5	Green
	12.5	Green/Lutino	12.5	Green/Blue
	12.5	Green/Blue	12.5	Lutino
	12.5	Green/Blue/Lutino	12.5	Lutino/Blue
Green/Blue/Lutino x Green/Blue	6.25	Green	6.25	Green
	12.5	Green/Blue	6.25	Lutino
	12.5	Green/Blue/Lutino	12.5	Lutino/Blue
	6.25	Blue	12.5	Green/Blue
	6.25	Blue/Lutino	6.25	Blue
	6.25	Green/Lutino	6.25	Albino
Green/Blue/Lutino x Lutino	12.5	Green/Lutino	12.5	Green
	12.5	Green/Blue/Lutino	12.5	Green/Blue
	12.5	Lutino	12.5	Lutino
	12.5	Lutino/Blue	12.5	Lutino/Blue
Green/Blue/Lutino x Lutino/Blue	6.25	Green/Lutino	6.25	Green
	12.5	Green/Blue/Lutino	12.5	Green/Blue
	6.25	Lutino	6.25	Lutino
	12.5	Lutino/Blue	12.5	Lutino/Blue
	6.25	Blue/Lutino	6.25	Blue
	6.25	Albino	6.25	Albino

Green/Blue/Lutino x Blue	12.5 12.5 12.5 12.5	Green/Blue Green/Blue/Lutino Blue Blue/Lutino	12.5 12.5 12.5 12.5	Green/Blue Blue Lutino/Blue Albino
Green/Blue/Lutino x Albino	12.5 12.5 12.5 12.5	Green/Blue/Lutino Lutino/Blue Blue/Lutino Albino	12.5 12.5 12.5 12.5	Green/Blue Lutino/Blue Blue Albino
Albino x Green	50	Green/Blue/Lutino	50	Lutino/Blue
Albino x Green/Blue	25 25	Green/Blue/Lutino Blue/Lutino	25 25	Lutino/Blue Albino
Albino x Lutino	50	Lutino/Blue	50	Lutino/Blue
Albino x Lutino/Blue	25 25	Lutino/Blue Albino	25 25	Lutino/Blue Albino
Albino x Blue	50	Blue/Lutino	50	Albino
Albino x Albino	50	Albino	50	Albino

The genetic inheritance of the various mutations are as follows:

Blue   - Recessive
Lutino - Sex-linked
Albino - Sex-linked
Grey   - Dominant

Genetic Inheritance
Sex-linked

In a sex-linked mutation, only the cock can be split for the mutant colour.

The hen is either Normal or the mutant colour.

Recessive

This type produces both cocks and hens split for the mutant colour.

Dominant

This mutant can affect either sex and is visual. Birds cannot be split for this colour eg. Grey-green or Grey. When two birds of a dominant mutation are mated, a percentage of the young will carry two factors. This difference will not be visual and can only be determined by test matings. This is why some birds are denoted as single or double factor.

The dominant Grey and Grey-green genes can occur in Single Factor (SF) and Double Factor (DF) forms. Their mode of inheritance is as follows:

SF x Normal   =   50% SF   50% Normal
SF x SF   =   50% SF   25% DF   25% Normal
SF x DF   =   50% SF   50% DF
DF x Normal   =   100% SF
DF x DF   =   100% DF

When one takes a close look at a Normal Indian Ringnecked Parrot, it is certainly not just a drab uniform green parrot. At least four different shades of green along with tones of blue and yellow within its makeup, has allowed the previous colours mentioned to be produced. Certainly an exquisite bird that will keep us busy for many years.

From left:
Lutino, Creamino, Turquoise and Blue Indian Ringnecked Parrots.

**Pair of
Alexandrine
Parrots**

K. WILSON

ALEXANDRINE PARROT

Psittacula eupatria

The Alexandrine Parrot is one of the largest of the Asiatic Parrots bred in Australian aviaries and because of its size, is not always suitable for every aviculturist. If you have a small backyard in suburban areas, they can be rather noisy, at times causing problems with neighbours who do not appreciate loud piercing bird calls.

However, a large percentage of aviculturists who live in open areas, where noise is not a problem, find Alexandrines to be an excellent bird. In fact, it has only been in fairly recent years that people have taken notice of them, prior to that we feel they were very underrated.

Like all Asiatic Parrots, rarely do you see one in poor feather condition, apart from when they are moulting. Alexandrine Parrots are an excellent example of a good feathered bird. Often

Above:
Alexandrine Parrot cock.

Right:
Pair of Alexandrine Parrots.

at bird shows the common remark from budgerigar breeders is ' how do you get a bird that size in perfect feather?' Our answer to that is, if they are housed properly, it just seems to be in their makeup.

People new to aviculture probably don't realise how lucky we are to have this species of bird available. Thirty years ago there were very few Alexandrine Parrots available, however, with careful breeding from dedicated aviculturists, Alexandrines have slowly progressed and are freely available today. There is rather a marked difference in the size of various Alexandrine Parrots you may see. Some believe that there is a large race and a small race of the species. However, in our experience we would simply describe the difference in size as being between the weak and the strong.

Sexing

A good sized cock Alexandrine Parrot should measure around 550-580mm (22-23 inches) in length, be rather bold in the head and stand firmly on the perch with an alert appearance. The hen is slightly shorter in the tail and has a rounder, more feminine head than the cock.

In selecting birds, particular attention should be made to size and the amount of chestnut red on the wing patch of both sexes. Some Alexandrine Parrots are very poorly coloured in this area.

Housing

The aviaries we use are of the open flight type as these birds benefit from access to rain. Regardless of the time of year, as soon as it is raining, Asiatic Parrots delight in hanging on the wire or sitting on the perch to get a good soaking. This is very beneficial, not only for maintaining good feather condition, but also it is a great help in egg hatchability, by supplying moisture to the eggs from the brooding hen's breast feathers.

Above: Pair of Alexandrine Parrots.
Left: Alexandrine Parrot eggs.

Alexandrines like to chew, therefore, an aviary built of galvanised pipe or box steel tube with heavy 16 gauge (1.6mm) weldmesh, is required. The aviary length should be at least 4.8 metres (16 feet) long x 1.2 metres (4 feet) wide x 2.1 metres (7 feet) high, one third of this shelter.

One pair per flight is suggested, however, in some cases colony breeding has been successful.

Being such large birds and heavy fliers, it is advisable to place a leafy branch or similar at either end of the flight that youngsters can crash land into, saving skinned heads or broken wings. Within a few days they soon settle down and are a sensible bird in a long flight.

Feeding

Feeding is as discussed in the general *Feeding* section.

During breeding, a basic diet of grey-striped sunflower seed, hulled oats and budgerigar mix is always available. A daily supply of green food such as milk thistle, oats in head and corn on the cob or boiled corn, whichever you are able to obtain, makes for an excellent supplement at this time. In our experience, if a daily supply of corn is not supplied, the parents are not able to keep up the food required from just a dry seed mix. Their diet does not include a lot of fruit, however, apples will readily be eaten.

Breeding

Alexandrine Parrots are generally excellent parents, usually rearing all their young without problems, provided the parents have adequate food available to feed the youngsters. If food supply is inadequate, rarely do they allow the young to die, as many other species would. They continue to rear the best they can, however on leaving the nest, the young are much smaller than they should be.

We never expect breeding success until both the cock and hen are at least three years old. From this age on we have found them to be

Alexandrine Parrot cocks and Lutino hen.

Above:
Lutino Alexandrine hen.

Right:
Alexandrine hybrid
Indian Ringnecked young
- 7/8 Alexandrine.

Below:
Lutino hen 3/4
Alexandrine (One week
after fledging). Note rust
coloured shoulder
patches on hybrid split
Lutino cock.

very reliable breeders usually going to nest, in southern Victoria, around the end of July.

Natural hollow logs, 900mm (3 feet) long with an inside diameter of 250-300mm (10-12 inches), hung vertically, are used for nesting. A 120mm (4.5 inches) diameter entrance hole is cut approximately 150mm (6 inches) from the top of the hollow. Logs of this size are rather heavy, therefore an inspection opening is made 230mm (9 inches) from the bottom. This allows the breeder to inspect without having to lift the log down. Natural rotted hardwood sawdust is used for the nesting chamber.

If logs are not available, a nestbox constructed of sawn timber or plyboard covered with flat iron, to restrict the birds from chewing, with a ladder of weldmesh or similar attached inside, would be suitable. It should measure approximately 250mm (10 inches) square x 900mm (3 feet) high.

Three to four eggs is a normal clutch and although the cock will enter the log, only the hen incubates.

Incubation lasts approximately 24 days and on hatching, young soon need a constant supply of food, which can be easily regurgitated by the parents.

Chicks stay in the nest for approximately seven to eight weeks. Young are independent a month after leaving the nest and we have never had to remove young from the parents' flight through bullying. It is a rare occasion for Alexandrines to double brood.

Most young Alexandrine cocks will show colour at 12 months of age, yet others do not show colour until 18 months. Usually they display a full neck ring of pink and black by the time they are two years old. Hens do not develop a neck ring, but will show the chestnut red wing patch.

Mutation

In an effort to produce Lutino Alexandrines, some breeders have hybridised pure or Normal Alexandrines with Lutino Indian Ringnecked Parrots. However, it is a long programme and care must be taken to keep thorough records of matings and hybrids. The end result is an outstanding mutation, well worth the effort if properly managed. Green hybrids, especially in the first cross, tend to show a more rust coloured shoulder patch than the pure Alexandrine.

We began some 15 years ago by mating a Normal green Alexandrine cock to a Lutino Indian Ringnecked hen. The offspring from this mating produces all visual Green youngsters, the cocks being split for Lutino. The hens are disregarded as they do not carry the Lutino gene. These split cocks are then paired to Normal Alexandrine hens which produce Lutino hens and possibly split cocks.

Each generation must be mated to Normal Alexandrines so that size and conformation is improved. After four generations we have been able to produce Lutino Alexandrines that are as good as the Normal greens.

One must have patience, time and plenty of aviary space if contemplating a challenge such as this, however, it is well worth the effort.

A quicker way of producing Lutinos is to mate a cock Lutino Indian Ringnecked Parrot to Normal Alexandrine hen. The progeny are Green cocks split for Lutino and Lutino hens, however birds bred from this mating often lack size and usually run into fertility problems.

PLUM-HEADED PARROT
Psittacula cyanocephala cyanocephala

K. WILSON

Plum-headed Parrot hens differ from Blossom-headed hens by having no red bar on the shoulders and the tip of the tail is white instead of yellow.

The Plum-headed Parrot was added to our collection of parrots in 1962 and is a definite favourite.

They are reasonably reliable breeders adapting to either a hot or cold climate. Originating from a hot country, Plum-headed Parrots have coped exceptionally well in the colder climate of southern Victoria, not showing any signs of discomfort during the foggy, misty days that are often experienced.

Being a bird of only 330-350mm (13-14 inches) in length, the Plum-headed Parrot is a suitably sized bird that is not noisy, does not chew and is extremely attractive and colourful.

Sexing

They have been well named, for if you were to describe the colouring of an adult cock, the most striking feature is the head, which is a very rich deep red to plum colour, being separated from the green body colour by a distinct black neck ring. A chestnut shoulder patch is also present. The hen is duller in colour with a green body and grey head. The hen also has a yellowish band around the neck and lacks the chestnut shoulder patch.

Sexing young birds is extremely difficult. At what age these birds can be sexed depends on how early in the season the youngsters fledge. Young that fly early in November often show signs of colour when two years of age but do not fully colour until three years old. However, young that fledge in late December/early January do not show any signs of colour until their third year and then, within weeks, the cocks completely colour.

Surgical sexing has been a great breakthrough for aviculture and avian veterinarians have become very experienced in this field, so breeders or buyers can have young sexed to save the long wait of wondering.

Plum-headed Parrot
cock.

Plum-headed cock.

Plum-headed cocks.

Housing

Housing for these birds is fairly simple. Being a small bird they only require an aviary 3-3.6 metres (10-12 feet) long x 900mm (3 feet) wide x 2.1 metres (7 feet) high, a third of the length being shelter. The aviary frame can be constructed of timber, as the birds do not chew and either 12mm (l/2 inch) bird wire or weldmesh can be used on the open flight.

Plum-headed Parrots are best kept as a single pair per flight, however we have housed Bourke's Parrots with them with no problems. In planted aviaries they really show themselves off flying amongst the greenery and not interfering with finches or doves.

Feeding

Feeding requirements are as described under the general *Feeding* section.

Breeding

The breeding of Plum-headed Parrots depends on compatibility of the pairs. Some hens can be aggressive towards their partners, often taking control of the perch and bullying the cock until a few weeks before egg laying. This often results in poor fertility. However, in compatible pairs the hen does not do this at all, forming a pair bond, with feeding and mating taking place many times before egg laying.

Nest logs or nestboxes can be used, although they prefer a small log with an inside diameter of around 150mm (6 inches) approximately 380mm (15 inches) long with a small entrance hole 38-50mm (1.5-2 inches) in diameter. A suitable nestbox size is 180mm (7 inches) square x 450mm (18 inches) high.

Plum-headed hen in her log. Note how she curls her tail over her back.

Plum-headed Parrots have a bad habit of removing sawdust from the nest log and it is surprising how quickly they are able to do this. Weekly inspections should be made to check that all sawdust is not removed, otherwise the hen will start laying on the bare bottom of the nest log or nestbox. If a hen keeps rearranging the material, it is just a matter of replacing it with more moist hardwood sawdust, and ramming this down tightly with your fist. Continue to replace sawdust until she stops. Once egg laying commences, they seem to be satisfied with the nesting chamber and rarely cart any more out.

The normal clutch usually consists of four to five eggs and incubation lasts approximately 23 days. All the young hatch together. The parents are very devoted to their young, with the hen leaving the nest to be fed by the cock regularly throughout the day, returning to feed the youngsters. Plum-headed Parrots have a reputation for letting young die after about three weeks of age. This has been overcome by keeping up a daily supply of boiled corn and seeding grasses along with their regular supply of dry seed consisting of grey-striped sunflower seed, budgerigar mix and hulled oats.

On fledging, some seven weeks after hatching, young are a very plain green with pale yellow beaks, not looking anywhere near as colourful as their parents. After the first moult, at around three months of age, the green head changes to a silvery grey colour. They retain this colour for at least two years and from then on cocks can show odd red feathers, either on the head or where the wing patch will further develop.

The adult hens, over eight to ten years of age, sometimes show a few red feathers on the head, the numbers increasing as they grow older. Inexperienced bird keepers may think they are young cocks just colouring up. The beak of the adult hen is a much duller orange yellow than the beak of the cock.

Plum-headed Parrots rarely have a successful second brood. We have tried fostering the first clutch of eggs under Indian Ringnecked Parrots and the hen will lay again, however infertile eggs often result, so it appears to be a wasted exercise, just exhausting the hen.

We find Plum-headed Parrots long lived with pairs in our collection breeding regularly for the past 15 years. One cock is at least 24 years old and one hen, 20 years old. Their numbers are steadily increasing in this country and being so popular they are often exported overseas.

Mutation

Mutations of Plum-headed Parrots in Australia are rare. We have a cock that has gradually, over the years, turned yellow whilst still retaining the red head. This is what is termed an 'acquired' colour. Efforts have been made to produce with him with little success.

Plum-headed Parrots are rather active birds in an aviary and if small twiggy branches are provided, cocks delight in sitting on the thinnest end, bobbing up and down displaying to their hens. A magnificent sight cementing their future in our collection.

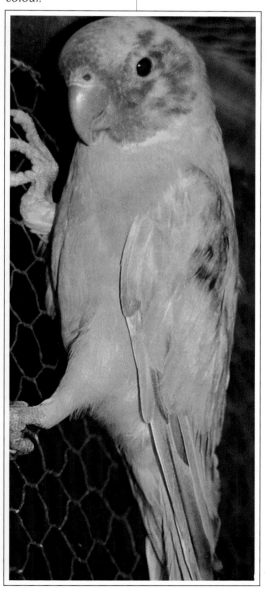

This Yellow or Pied cock Plum-headed Parrot has become yellower over the years and is thus termed an 'acquired' colour.

Pair of Slaty-headed Parrots.

SLATY-HEADED PARROT
Psittacula himalayana himalayana

The Slaty-headed Parrot has only recently been added to our collection. Until a few years ago, we considered this species to be not nearly as attractive as the Plum-headed Parrot. However, repeated enquiries and an obvious increase in demand for them, has led to us keeping a few pairs.

In peak condition they are a smart looking bird about 400mm (16 inches) in length. One of the most striking features is their long tail feathers which gives them a streamlined, slender appearance. However, if they are housed in small aviaries, the tails are often broken and this detracts from their appearance.

Pair of Slaty-headed Parrots with their young

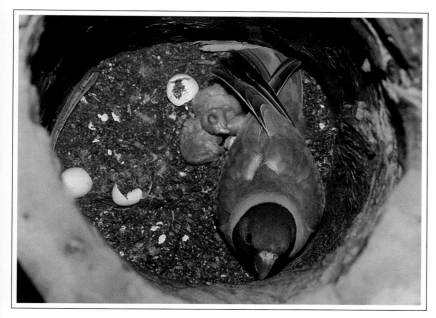

Slaty-headed hen in nesting log with young.

Pair of Slaty-headed Parrots.

Young Slaty-headed Parrots.

Sexing

We find that as the hen is about to commence nesting around August, the head turns a duller grey and the beak develops a chalky appearance. Both the cock and the hen are similar in appearance except the hen does not carry the maroon wing patch.

Housing

Housing for this species is similar to that of the Plum-headed Parrot. An aviary 3-3.6 metres (10-12 feet) long x 900mm (3 feet) wide x 2.1 metres (7 feet) high, a third of the length being shelter, is adequate. Weldmesh or 12mm (1/2 inch) bird wire can be used on the open flights.

Feeding

Feeding this species is as described under the general *Feeding* section, using the basic seed mix and plenty of milk thistle and corn on the cob when breeding. Slaty-headed Parrots will also readily eat fruit.

Breeding

Slaty-headed Parrots have a good reputation for rearing their own young right through without any problems, not usually needing to be taken from the nest and handreared or fostered under other species. Being slightly larger than the Plum-headed Parrot in size, a nest log of approximately 200mm (8 inches) in diameter and 450mm (18 inches) to 600mm (24 inches) long is required. Nestboxes 200mm (8 inches) square x 450mm (18 inches) to 600mm (24 inches) high are ideal. Hens settle down quicker than Plum-heads, not removing sawdust from the log and often adding down feathers once egg laying commences. They are also very tolerant when their nest is inspected. Clutches of four to five eggs are not uncommon. Incubation lasts approximately 24 days and young stay in the nest for around seven weeks. On fledging, the young are a rather uninteresting green. Like Plum-headed Parrots, they go into a moult and the head colour changes to grey at around six months. Often, at this age the odd black feathers appear on the neck ring and at 15 to 18 months one is able to sex cocks from hens. Adult plumage is acquired at two to two and a half years of age.

On weaning, young Slaty-heads are housed together in a holding aviary where they show no signs of aggression towards one another.

BLOSSOM-HEADED PARROT
Psittacula cyanocephala rosa

There are still a number of Blossom-headed Parrots which are held by a few experienced aviculturists, in Australia, so hopefully they will increase in numbers. Possibly the reason the Blossom-headed Parrot is not as common in aviaries today is the price difference between this species and the Plum-headed Parrot. Many people are attracted by the value and colour of a species. A comparison could also be made between our native Cloncurry Parrot and Mallee Ringnecked Parrot. It is not generally understood how similar looking birds can vary so much in price.

The Blossom-headed Parrot is slightly smaller than the Plum-headed Parrot, being approximately 300mm (12 inches) in length. Their colouration is also very similar. For all intent and purposes their basic requirements are almost identical to that of the Plum-headed Parrot.

Blossom-headed Parrot cock.

Sexing
The main colouration difference between the Plum-heads and the Blossom-heads is that the cock Blossom-headed Parrot displays more of a pink colour on the head, not developing the plum colour of the Plum-headed Parrot. The hen Blossom-headed Parrot has a maroon patch on the wing, which is lacking in the hen Plum-headed Parrot. Both the hen's and the cock's tails are tipped with yellow, whereas this is white in Plum-heads.

Housing
The aviary requirements for Blossom-headed Parrots are the same as for Plum-headed Parrots. An aviary 3-3.6 metres (10-12 feet) long

x 900mm (3 feet) wide x 2.1 metres (7 feet) high, a third of the length being shelter, would be ideal. This small, gentle parrot can also be kept in a mixed collection with finches and doves, however, for optimum breeding results one pair per aviary is recommended.

Feeding

Feeding requirements are as described under the general *Feeding* section and are similar to those of the Plum-headed Parrot.

Breeding

Whilst this species are ready breeders, it is rare, as with other Asiatic Parrots, for a second or third clutch. The hen can be noticeably aggressive towards her mate, although this does not necessarily affect breeding results.

Generally, four and occasionally five eggs per clutch are laid. Incubation lasts approximately 23 days. A nest log with an internal diameter of 150mm (6 inches) and about 380mm (15 inches) long, with an entrance hole 50mm (2 inches) in diameter, is preferred. If a nestbox is provided, it should be 180mm (7 inches) square x 450mm (18 inches) high.

Blossom-heads will readily hybridise with Plum-headed Parrots and it would take a trained eye to detect these hybrids. Hopefully, breeders will retain the integrity of this species.

DERBYAN PARROT
Psittacula derbyana

Having only seen photographs and paintings of Derbyan Parrots, our minds were completely changed the first time we experienced these magnificent birds in the feather. We immediately went in search of obtaining this species.

Pair of Derbyan Parrots, hen on right.

The feature that took our eye was the deep purple breast of these large birds, which is a colour you do not see on many parrots. They also have a strong head with an alert eye and this seems to really set them off. Although they have the same body size as an Alexandrine Parrot, the tail is not as long which gives them a stocky appearance. The overall length is approximately 500mm (20 inches).

Sexing
The Derbyan Parrot can be visually sexed at approximately eight months of age. Young fledge at approximately eight weeks of age. They are as large as their parents but duller in colour with red beaks. At three months, the beak colour changes to black and then at eight months, the cock develops a red beak whilst the hen's beak remains black.

One also gets an indication of sex by the presence of a pink line on the neck when the young are in the log. The cock lacks this colour. However, some hens do not show as much pink as others, so we only use this as a guide. Certainly the beak colour is more accurate.

Pair of Derbyans - cock on left.

Derbyan hen at nest entrance.

Housing

Derbyan Parrots spend a lot of time chewing and can be very destructive. Perches need replacing regularly and the aviary frame needs to be constructed of box steel tube or galvanised pipe with heavy gauge weldmesh wire.

Derbyans are best housed in single pairs in open flight aviaries 5.4 metres (18 feet) long x 2.1 metres (7 feet) high x 1.2 metres (4 feet) wide, a third of this being shelter.

Feeding

We find the feeding of Derbyans, unlike other Asiatic species, a problem. We have had arguments with other breeders over the suitability of sunflower seed. Some say it is a drug with birds becoming addicted to it and that it can also cause feather problems. We totally disagree with this for if you did not feed sunflower seed to this species you would soon have some very dead Derbyans.

We have tried feeding all types of parrot seed mixes and grey-striped sunflower seed is virtually all we can get them to regularly eat. Even with green feed they are not too keen but they will eat apples or either boiled corn or fresh corn cobs hung in the aviary. After generations of breeding Derbyans, we have tried to entice young to take more greens but with little success.

Only on one occasion have we seen a poorly feathered Derbyan Parrot. This bird had been handraised and obviously had not been fed a suitable handrearing mixture, as it was undersized and a poor specimen overall.

Fortunately, Derbyan Parrot numbers are increasing in Australia and although still expensive, good parrot collections are usually represented with this species.

Breeding

Some aviculturists have not experienced much success breeding this Asiatic species. However, in our experience, we have found them to be regular breeders, preferring a cold rather than hot climate.

A nest log 900mm (3 feet) long should be provided with an inside diameter of 250-300mm (10-12 inches). A large opening of at least 130mm (5 inches) in diameter is suggested, as these birds nest some six weeks later than other Asiatic species and by the time young are ready to leave the nest we are starting to

Above: Derbyan chicks approximately six weeks old.
Left: Young Derbyan two days after fledging - note red beak at this stage.
Below: Derbyan chick approximately four weeks old - note heavy down.

Above   A striking comparison between Derbyan cock (left) and cock Moustache.

experience hot weather with temperatures during the day up to 38°C (100°F). If there is not enough air circulation in the nest, young can become dehydrated. If temperatures rise over 29°C (85°F), regular inspections of the chicks should be made. One can put the chicks in an open topped box on the floor of the aviary through the day, returning them to the log at night with no problems. Derbyans are most tolerant of this interference.

Not usually breeding until three years old and with a small clutch size of two to three eggs, nobody will mass produce this species. We have pairs over 20 years old breeding regularly so they do have a long lifespan.

Most Asiatic species are born bald, not so with Derbyan chicks. After 24 days of incubation, young hatch with yellowish down, much like a Homing Pigeon. This is replaced with a dense dark grey down like the Eclectus, giving them the appearance of a baby penguin.

Derbyan Parrot cock.

MOUSTACHE PARROT

Psittacula alexandri fasciata

Moustache Parrot cock (right) with young, one week after fledging. Note, young bird's bill is red at this stage.

Purchasing all stock of this species from the late Mr Joe Mattinson's collection in April 1988, our experience with this species to date is rather limited. However, in this short time, we find they are very similar to the Derbyan Parrot except they are only half the size and not as fussy eaters.

When being caught, they roll over in the hand net on their backs, squeaking continually, exactly as Derbyans do.

Another point of interest we have noticed, is that after the breeding season, the hen hides in the nest log until about July when she gives this unusual behaviour away, spending more time out on the perch. We have no explanation for this behaviour. The cock rarely enters the log.

Sexing

Sexing of Moustache Parrots is the same as with Derbyan Parrots. The young cock's beak colour changes from black to a bright red at eight months of age. The hen's beak colour remains black.

Moustache Parrots have rather a plump body with a reasonably short tail compared with other Asiatic species. Total length is approximately 330mm (13 inches). Both the adult cock and the hen are very similar in colour. The main difference is the beak colour, red in the cock and black in the hen.

Housing

Large aviaries are not necessary and ideally a single pair are housed per flight. Aviaries measuring 3.0-3.6 metres (10-12 feet) long x 900mm (3 feet) wide x 2.1 metres (7 feet) high, a third of this being shelter, are ideal. Although not chewing as much as Derbyans, a heavy gauge bird wire or weldmesh is suggested.

Feeding

Feeding habits are rather different from Derbyans as although they eat large amounts of grey-striped sunflower seed, they will also eat the smaller seeds in the budgerigar mix. Hulled oats are eagerly consumed when young are in the nest. Green feed in the form of milk thistle and oats in head hung in the flight, are a great favourite.

Breeding

Nest logs, hung vertically, measuring 600mm (2 feet) long with an inside diameter of 200mm (8 inches) and an entrance hole of 50mm (2 inches) diameter, are preferred.

Above: Moustache Parrot cock.
Left: Moustache Parrot hen.
Below: Moustache Parrot cock.

Above:
Moustache chicks
approximately three
days old.

Right:
Moustache
immatures. Bird on
right has red eyes -
possibly a Fallow
mutant.

Below:
Young Moustache
Parrots.

The hen spends a lot of time in the nest log before egg laying commences. However, once settled, she lays a clutch of three to four eggs, which is rather large for the size of the bird. The hen sits tight, only leaving the nest early in the morning or late in the afternoon to feed herself or be fed by the cock.

On nest inspections, the hen is very hard to persuade to move off her eggs. Incubation lasts for approximately 21-24 days. These birds are excellent parents, with the young growing rapidly over the seven weeks they are in the nest. On fledging, young are sensible, not flying erratically as most Asiatic youngsters often do.

Full adult plumage is attained after 15 months.

Subspecies

There is also a subspecies of Moustache Parrot, *P.a. alexandri*. The hen is identical to the cock except for a faint pink line on the neck directly behind the black moustache. This race is rather aggressive towards one another. The more common race *P. a. fasciato* are very compatible towards each other and young are able to be kept with their parents until they colour.

Moustache Parrot hen.

MALABAR PARROT
Psittacula columboides

The Malabar Parrot has always been rare in Australian aviaries. Our first sighting of these birds was in the early 1960's, in the aviaries of the late Mr Joe Mattinson of Wollongong, New South Wales. Apart from these few pairs, to our knowledge, there were very few in other collections.

Other than being expensive, Malabar Parrots have a reputation for feather plucking, a contributing factor as to why we had not added this species to our collection earlier.

In the first edition of this book we made mention of the Malabar Parrot, however, not having kept them, our knowledge was limited. Breeders requested more information, so in the early 1990s we set about procuring some young stock, to establish breeding pairs.

Sexing

The Malabar Parrot has a body size similar to the Moustache Parrot with a slightly longer tail, overall length being approximately 380mm (15 inches).

The head and body colour is bluish grey with the back feathers laced with yellow-gold. Like all cock Asiatic Parrots, a distinct black ring encircles the neck. Behind this ring, is a turquoise green colour which increases with age. This green colour also encircles the eyes in the cock. The hen Malabar Parrot does not display this turquoise green colour ring behind the black neck ring. The cock has a red beak and the hen a black beak.

The accompanying colour photographs show their colouring in much fuller detail.

Pair of Malabar Parrots.

Malabar hen.

Housing

Travelling many kilometres inspecting other breeder's Malabars, we realised that many of the birds that were in poor feather were either housed in small suspended cages or in aviaries that were completely roofed, denying the occupants access to rain and in some cases even sunshine.

Birds housed in outdoor flight aviaries were generally free of feather problems. Also, birds kept in a cooler climate were in better condition than those kept in hotter areas. It was obvious a large percentage of Malabar Parrot problems was due to mismanagement and not necessarily the fault of the bird.

An aviary 3-3.6 metres (10-12 feet) long x 900mm (3 feet) wide x 2.1 metres (7 feet) high, a third of the length being shelter, is suggested. The aviary framing can be constructed from timber as Malabar Parrots do not chew. Weldmesh or 12mm (1/2 inch) bird wire should be used on the open flight.

Feeding

Feeding requirements are as described under the general *Feeding* section and are similar to those for the Slaty-headed and Plum-headed Parrot.

Breeding

Nesting requirements are similar to that of the Slaty-headed and Plum-headed Parrot.

Both the cock and the hen regularly display to one another, rolling and dilating their eyes. They are very protective of their nest, flying from perch to nest log and often mating in full view when one approaches their aviary.

Malabar cock.

Eggs are laid every second day and incubation commences when the last egg is laid. Three to four eggs is an average clutch. With only the hen incubating, young can be expected to hatch approximately 24 days later.

Parents are very attentive and can be relied on to raise their young with no problems.

Fledging some seven to eight weeks later, young are a duller version of their parents with the main point of interest being that their beaks are a bright red. The beak colour soon changes to black and remains so until eight months of age, when it reverts back to red in the cock. The hen's beak remains black. At the first complete moult at 12 months, much of the colouring is evident, this improving when the young are fully coloured at two years of age, when

displaying and nesting can be expected.

Although we have never handraised a Malabar Parrot chick, we would imagine they would make an excellent pet. Adults and parent reared young have an inbuilt cheekiness and will continually come to the front of the aviary looking for attention.

The quietness of these birds is also noted, as on leaving the nest, young do not fly erratically, as do some other Asiatic species. With this natural quietness, they are less prone to night and day frights from outside predators and can handle stress a little better than some other species when being transported.

In the short term, we have found Malabar Parrots to be as hardy as other Asiatic Parrot species and regret not including them in our collection earlier.

Above: Malabar chicks approximately ten days old.

Right: Malabar immatures with cock parent.

Below: Malabar immature (three weeks out of the nest).

P. ODEKERKEN

MALAYAN LONG-TAILED PARROT
Psittacula longicauda

Malayan Long-tailed Parrots came into our collection in the early 1960s when four uncoloured birds were purchased from a Melbourne dealer.

The general mangement of this species is similar to the Slaty-headed Parrot.

Sexing

In adult plumage, the cocks live up to their name as they have two distinct very long blue tail feathers which look out of proportion to the body size. The hen's tail is a much more sensible length. The cock is predominantly green with a thick black moustache and red cheeks. The beak is red. The hen has duller red cheeks, a green moustache and the beak is black. The cock is approximately 400mm (16 inches) in length.

Housing

In its natural habitat the Malayan Long-tailed Parrot prefers open country or the fringe of high jungle. Being a swift flyer and continuously active, it is suggested that a relatively medium to large aviary be supplied. An aviary 3.5-4 metres (12-13 feet) long x 900 mm (3 feet) wide x 2.1 metres (7 feet) high, would be adequate, a third of the length being shelter. Although a colony bird in the wild, for maximum breeding potential, one pair per aviary is recommended.

Feeding

Feeding requirements are as described under the general *Feeding* section, with the exception that this species requires a much larger daily supply of fruit.

Breeding

These are a specialist bird with very few breeding successes recorded. Nest logs or nestboxes can be used. Logs should have a minimum diameter of 150mm (6 inches), approximately 400mm (16 inches) long with an entrance hole of about 50mm (2 inches) in diameter. A suitable nestbox size is 180mm (7 inches) square x 450mm (18 inches) high. A clutch of two to three eggs is laid. Incubation lasts approximately 24 days. Only the hen incubates.

In retrospect, we regret having exchanged our Malayan Long-tailed Parrots for other species. There are few available in Australia currently. We can only hope that through intensive management and careful use of the gene pool we have available, these birds can be saved for future Australian aviculturists to enjoy.

The Acclaimed 'A Guide to...' series.

■ A Guide to Australian Grassfinches

The popularity of Australian Grassfinches worldwide is largely due to the hardiness of these tiny, gregarious and colourful birds. Some 18 species of Grassfinch that are all members of the family Estrildae are recognised in Australia. General topics covered include - Acquiring Birds, Quarantine, Nutrition, Housing, Compatibility and Regulating the Breeding Season, to name just a few. A must for every Finch breeders' library.

ISBN NUMBER 0 9587102 28 Author: Russell Kingston

■ A Guide to Neophema and Psephotus Grass Parrots and Their Mutations (Revised Edition)

Bourke's Parrot, Turquoisine Parrot, Scarlet-chested Parrot, Elegant Parrot, Blue-winged Parrot, Rock Parrot, Orange-bellied Parrot, Red-rumped Parrot, Mulga Parrot, Blue-bonnet, Hooded Parrot, Golden-shouldered Parrot and Paradise Parrot.

ISBN NUMBER 0 9587102 44 Author: Toby Martin

■ A Guide to Asiatic Parrots and Their Mutations (Revised Edition)

Alexandrine Parrot, Plum-headed Parrot, Indian Ringnecked Parrot, Derbyan Parrot, Malabar Parrot, Slaty-headed Parrot, Malayan Long-tailed Parrot, Blossom-headed Parrot and Moustache Parrot.

ISBN NUMBER 0 9587102 52 Authors: Syd & Jack Smith

■ A Guide to Australian Long and Broad-tailed Parrots and New Zealand Kakarikis

Crimson-winged Parrot, Princess Parrot, Regent Parrot, Superb Parrot, King Parrot, Red-capped Parrot, Mallee Ringnecked Parrot, Cloncurry Parrot, Port Lincoln Parrot, Twenty-eight Parrot, Red-fronted Parrot and Yellow-fronted Parrot.

ISBN NUMBER 0 9587455 36 Author: Kevin Wilson

■ A Guide to Rosellas and Their Mutations

Eastern Rosella, Tasmania Eastern Rosella, Golden-mantled Rosella, Pale-headed Rosella, Blue-cheeked Rosella, Northern Rosella, Kimberley Northern Rosella, Western Rosella, Red-backed Western Rosella, Crimson Rosella, Northern Crimson Rosella, Yellow Rosella, Adelaide Rosella, Tasmanian Rosella.

ISBN NUMBER 0 9587455 52 Author: Australian Birdkeeper

■ A Guide to Eclectus Parrots

A comprehensive look at the keeping, breeding, housing, health and management of these beautiful parrots, including hand-rearing tips.

ISBN NUMBER 0 9587455 44 Author: Australian Birdkeeper

■ A Guide to Gouldian Finches and Their Mutations

Covers all requirements to successfully breed and maintain Gouldians including concise information on health, nutrition and colour mutations.

ISBN NUMBER 0 9587455 60
Authors: John Sammut & Dr Rob Marshall

■ A Guide to Cockatiels and Their Mutations

Written by two of Australia's foremost Cockatiel breeders, the book features beautiful colour photography, including all known mutations. Excellent easy-to-read information covers the care, management, housing and breeding of these popular birds.

ISBN NUMBER 0 9587455 87
Authors: Peggy Cross and Diana Andersen

■ A Guide to Pigeons, Doves and Quail

A world first in aviculture, this book covers all species in this group available to the Australian aviculturist. Stunning colour photography throughout is supported by precise, easy-to-read information on the care, management, health and breeding of these unique birds.

ISBN NUMBER 0 6462305 81 Author: Danny Brown

■ A Guide to Lories and Lorikeets

Recognised internationally as a specialist lory/lorikeet breeder, Peter Odekerken is perhaps best known for his superb photography of which he probably has the most definitive collection of lory/lorikeet photographic studies in the world today. This new, long-awaited title in the acclaimed 'A Guide to...' series exemplifies Peter's great love and understanding of these unique and colourful, brush-tongued psittacines.

ISBN NUMBER 0 9587445 95 Author: Peter Odekerken

■ A Guide to Basic Health and Disease in Birds

This addition to the internationally acclaimed 'A Guide to...' series is packed with valuable user-friendly information that every birdkeeper should have at their side. From finches to macaws, Mike discusses common diseases to be aware of, quarantine procedures, recognising health problems, to basic steps required to maintain healthy birds. A must for novice and experienced aviculturists alike.

ISBN NUMBER 0 6462305 73 Author: Dr Mike Cannon

■ A Guide to Incubation & Handraising Parrots

This title covers all the necessary requirements needed to successfully take an egg through to a fully weaned chick. Beautifully illustrated with colour images throughout, this valuable title also includes many charts and diagrams and informative text laid out in the easy-to-read format. An invaluable reference for any serious bird breeder.

ISBN NUMBER 0 9587102 1 X Author: Phil Digney

■ A Guide to Pheasants & Waterfowl

Author of the highly regarded A Guide to Pigeons, Doves & Quail, Dr Danny Brown has produced this superlative new title on pheasants and waterfowl. The informative easy-to-read text is lavishly supported with beautiful colour images throughout. Covering all aspects of caring, housing, management and breeding of these unique birds, this new title is a credit to the author and an ideal reference source.

ISBN 0 9587102 36   Author: Dr Danny Brown

■ A Guide to Pet and Companion Birds

This informative and often amusing 'introduction to bird keeping' appeals not only to the novice or want-to-be bird keeper, but also to the seasoned aviculturist looking for a refresher on the basics. Based on the authors' combined thirty years of bird keeping experience, this guide walks you through the process of selecting a bird right for you, caring for that bird, and understanding its behaviour.

ISBN 0 9587266 12   Authors: Ray Dorge and Gail Sibley

Handbook of
Birds, Cages & Aviaries

This handbook provides a complete overview to the selection, keeping, management and care of both pet and aviary birds from individual pets to larger aviary complexes. Topics include Choosing your Bird, Choosing and Keeping Pet Birds, Housing and Keeping Aviary Birds, Aviary Design, Construction and Management, Plantscaping your Aviary, Nutrition and Feeding, Breeding and Husbandry, General Management and Health and Disease Aspects. A must for the novice and serious aviculturist and all pet bird owners.

ISBN 0 9587102 95   Edited by: ABK Publications

Publisher's Note

This title is published by **ABK Publications** who produce a wide and varied range of avicultural literature including the world acclaimed **Australian Birdkeeper** magazine - a full colour, bi-monthly magazine specifically designed for birdlovers and aviculturists. It is the intention of the publishers to produce high quality, informative literature for birdlovers, fanciers and aviculturists alike throughout the world. It is also the publisher's belief that the dissemination of qualified information on the care, keeping and breeding of birds is imperative for the total well-being of captive birds and the increased knowledge of aviculturists.

Nigel Steele-Boyce

Nigel Steele-Boyce
Publisher/Editor-In-Chief
ABK Publications

For further information or FREE catalogue on any of ABK Publications quality products/publications write to:

ABK Publications
PO Box 6288
South Tweed Heads
NSW 2486 Australia
or
Phone: (07) 5590 7777 Fax: (07) 5590 7130
Email: birdkeeper@birdkeeper.com.au
http://www.birdkeeper.com.au